"Every once in a while you read a book that changes the way you look at life, but it is so rare to find a book that changes the way you *live* your life. *The Miracle Morning* does both, and faster than you ever thought possible."

**—Tim Sanders, former Chief Solutions Officer at Yahoo!
NY Times Bestselling Author, *Love Is the Killer App***

"I've always been a night owl so the idea of creating a morning routine was never an option and didn't appeal to me. Things were already going well with my current schedule, so why fix it if it's not broken? But I kept hearing about how valuable people's morning routines are to their success, their mood, and their lives. So, I made a commitment to give *The Miracle Morning* a shot. I've been doing it for over a year, and already I'm seeing massive changes in my focus, in my mood and in how much I'm able to get done."

**—Pat Flynn, Author of *Will It Fly?* and Host of the
#1 rated *Smart Passive Income* Podcast**

"I never thought I would say this about a "morning book," but *The Miracle Morning* CHANGED MY LIFE. Yes, you read that correctly. For years I've told myself 'I'm not a morning person' and for the most part, it was true. In fact, one of my WHYs for wanting to be an entrepreneur was my desire to sleep in. No alarm clock. No getting up at dark. I wanted to wake up when I wanted to wake up. When I started reading this, I was curious to see if it could break my strong narrative and my strong why. It did. After reading this book I actually started getting up at 4:00 a.m. and hitting the gym. Yes, you read the right—FOUR FREAKING A.M. As a result, my days are far more productive and my physique is changing before my eyes. I never thought I could be one of these weirdoes who get up at 4 a.m. Now I'm one of those weirdoes. I do it five times a week, and mostly without an alarm clock."

**—MJ DeMarco, Former CEO of Limos.com and
#1 Bestselling Author, *The Millionaire Fastlane***

"To read *The Miracle Morning* is to give yourself the gift of waking up each day to your full potential. It's time to stop putting off creating the life you want and deserve to live. Read this book and find out how."

—Dr. Ivan Misner, CEO and Founder of BNI®

"Hal Elrod is more than an inspiration. He has taken his incredible story and turned it into lessons that you can use to create your own miracles."

—Jeffrey Gitomer, NY Times Bestselling Author, *The Sales Bible*

"*The Miracle Morning* is the ONE thing that can make immediate and profound changes in any—or *every* area of your life. If you want your life to improve NOW, I highly recommend reading this book immediately."

"As a speaker, author, and business marketing consultant, I see the biggest thing holding people back from achieving the success they want is not that they don't know what to do; it's finding the *time* and *motivation* to do what they know. Hal Elrod has literally solved this problem. *The Miracle Morning* gives you the time and motivation you need to create the success you want, no matter how busy you are. I highly, highly recommend it."

—James Malinchak, featured on ABC's hit TV show *Secret Millionaire*, co-author of *Chicken Soup for the College Soul* and Founder of www.MillionaireSpeakerSecrets.com

"At first I thought Hal had lost his mind—why on earth would anyone get up so early *on a regular basis*?!?! I was skeptical… until I tried it. When I implemented Hal's strategies I noticed an immediate difference in my personal and professional life. *The Miracle Morning* will show you how to take control of your life, regardless of your past. I highly recommend it."

—Josh Shipp, TV host, Author, and Teen Behavior Expert

"Reading Hal's first book, *Taking Life Head On*, completely changed the way I live each day, and I've been waiting patiently for his next book. All I can say is that *The Miracle Morning* was definitely worth the wait! Hal gives us the blueprint for creating the success, happiness and prosperity that may have eluded us, and he's made it so simple that anyone can turn their life around—no matter what their circumstances."

—Debra Poneman, Co-author of *Chicken Soup for the American Idol® Soul* and Founder of Yes to Success, Inc.

"*The Miracle Morning* truly changed my life. It allowed me to start tapping into my full potential, which ultimately led me to a path of expanded consciousness that continues to reveal new opportunities and abilities."

—Nick Conedera, Film Director, *SHARP: The World's Finest Movie*

"*The Miracle Morning* is the most paradigm-shifting book since *The 4-Hour Workweek*. Hal lives and breathes the habits that he teaches, and this book will show you how to take your life and business to the next level."

—Brad Weimert, CEO of *Easy Pay Direct*, EasyPayDirect.com

"If you are ready to leave mediocrity behind you and maximize your potential, read this book, plain and simple. *The Miracle Morning* gives you the key to unlock your personal power and tap into the abilities that allow ordinary people to become extraordinary."

—Gail Lynne Goodwin, Founder of InspireMeToday.com

"*The Miracle Morning* is literally the ONE thing that changes EVERYTHING for people. I recommend it to all of my *Game Changers* coaching members, and I

COACHING VOLLEYBALL:
A SURVIVAL GUIDE FOR YOUR FIRST SEASON

By Whitney Bartiuk

Copyright © 2016 by Whitney L. Bartiuk

All rights reserved. This book or any portion thereof may not be reproduced or used in any manner whatsoever without the express written permission of the author except for the use of brief quotations in a book review.

Visit the author's website for volleyball coaches at www.getthepancake.com.

ISBN: 9781520790954

ACKNOWLEDGMENTS

If you think writing a book is easy, you haven't tried to write one!

First I would like to thank my parents, Bill and Colleen, for taking the time to read and edit my work multiple times… Even on their anniversary weekend! Your feedback helped immensely and I'm so thankful that you were both so invested in helping me finish this undertaking. Your editing skills and new ideas were very appreciated.

Next I need to thank my brother and my friends from Bowling Green for their encouragement to pursue my true passion and for helping me see that I would regret not making the decision to go down the road I am now on. I spent months talking about "maybes" and "what-ifs," and you all helped move me to action. Tyler, Jess, Jacob, and Kevin, you make a great support team and

I hope you feel that the support is returned.

Finally, I owe a tremendous amount of thanks to my husband, Maks. Not only do you encourage my grand plans, you also help me see how I can make them a reality. You let me dream, but then make me focus. This book is the first step towards my bigger plan, and it wouldn't have been written without you. I love you.

TABLE OF CONTENTS

INTRODUCTION 1

CHAPTER 1: DECIDING TO COACH..7

   Making The Decision 7

   Coaching Philosophy 8

   What Level To Coach 11

   Which Position: Head Or Assistant Coach 19

   Where To Coach 22

   Getting Your Foot In The Door 24

   Expectations 26

CHAPTER 2: PRESEASON PREPARATION..31

   Meet Your New Boss 31

   Paperwork, Paperwork, Paperwork 35

   Buy Equipment 38

CHAPTER 3: TRYOUTS 41

   Setup 41

   Skills To Test For 44

Testing Designs 45

Making Decisions 52

Announcing Your Team 55

CHAPTER 4: BEGINNING OF THE SEASON 61

Meeting The Parents 62

More Paperwork 66

Building Trust And Culture 71

Discipline 80

Practice Design 84

CHAPTER 5: YOUR FIRST MATCH OR TOURNAMENT 89

A Few Practicalities: Fees, Parking, Weather, & More 90

Warm-Ups 94

Lineups 97

Playing Time 100

Refereeing 103

CHAPTER 6: MAKING DECISIONS THROUGH DATA 109

The Art Of Keeping Stats 110

You Have Data… Now What? 113

Improvement Through Data 115

Data-Driven Drill Design 116

Constant Tracking 119

CHAPTER 7: MID-SEASON REFLECTION 121

Keep An Eye Out For Burnout 122

Team And Individual Progress 124

Check-In With Higher Ups 126

Refresh Drills 128

CHAPTER 8: MAJOR END OF THE YEAR EVENTS 131

Prep Work 133

Over-Communicate With Families 135

Make It Special 136

A Warning: Keep Your Coaching Style Consistent... 138

CHAPTER 9: CELEBRATIONS AND AWARDS 143

Logistics... 144

Determining Awards (Hint: Your Stats Help!) 149

Positivity Only... 152

CHAPTER 10: FINAL THOUGHTS ... 155

Ups And Downs 156

Getting To Year Two 165

ABOUT THE AUTHOR 169

INTRODUCTION

I am so excited for you to read this. This book about coaching volleyball is really the resource I was looking for back when I started coaching in 2008, but couldn't find anywhere.

Search for "volleyball drills" and you'll come up with hundreds of thousands of sites and books dedicated to the topic (mine included!). Wading through articles named Top Ten Passing Drills for 6th Graders and Best Fun and Easy Serving Drills can be fun and exciting, but does it really prepare you to coach?

There is so much more to coaching than just running the perfect sequence of drills at practice, yet this is what most other resources focus on.

This book is different! The stresses you'll face throughout your first season won't come from parents not understanding why you're running a certain drill... It will come from parents parking in the wrong parking lot at your first tournament and then getting towed. And that will be a problem you're going to have to deal with.

Continuing this example, if you would have realized before your first tournament that you needed to send out logistical information like parking, entry fees, food policies, etc., your first tournament would have gone much more smoothly, and all you would have had to worry about would have been volleyball.

But this is so much more than just a step-by-step guide. It will get you thinking about your coaching philosophy right away and will take you from tryouts to awards and into your second season. You will be able to hone your coaching style and understand what your values are, making you a coach your players, families, and administrators can trust to get the job done.

You will also get pointers on how to keep the

season fun and exciting when you hit the ever-present mid-season slump. And keeping stats? You'll learn how to do that too. Even the basics, such as laying out ground rules from the very beginning, are often overlooked by first-year coaches.

These pages are filled with examples and illustrations of my suggestions, usually to highlight the importance of certain points. All of them have happened in real life, and I have either experienced them as a player, coach, referee, tournament director, or spectator. Most of the stories I am thankful to have experienced, whereas others I wish I wouldn't have seen.

My goal in writing this book is for you to access the material multiple times throughout the season and have the answers to your questions right at your fingertips. I want you to have confidence in your role in your first year coaching, whether that's as an assistant coach or a head coach.

Please keep in mind, however, that there is no way to include everything you may encounter in a season in one book. While I will share major learning points in my coaching career, you are not guaranteed to have the same experience. I have made my best effort to include all of the information you will need to know to have a successful season, but there are still situations which may arise that catch you off guard. My best advice to you is to read this guide before sitting down to discuss it with an administrator or head coach and rely on them for any additional information you may need.

So please, jump right in. Skip around if you are interested in reading about keeping stats before you dive into the preseason prep material. I recommend, however, starting with defining your coaching philosophy, which is referenced in several areas of this book (yes, it's that important). Some sections will have more of an impact on your success than others, but it is all important information. Regardless of your approach to reading this book, I ask two things.

First, if there is a section which asks you to brainstorm ideas or fill in the blanks, please do so. This will give you the most value.

Second, read all of the sections, even if you just

INTRODUCTION

skim the bullet points. I hate seeing things catch new coaches by surprise, and I want you to be prepared and to succeed. By buying this book, you clearly have an interest in being the best coach you can be in your first year, and I don't want you to get thrown for a loop at the end of your season when you change your coaching style because you didn't read that far.

Thank you, and I hope you enjoy.

CHAPTER 1: DECIDING TO COACH

MAKING THE DECISION

It takes a special personality to coach. Coaching requires a certain mixture of playfulness, competitiveness, patience, compassion, a desire to teach, and you must have great organizational skills to boot. Let's face it. Not everyone has these characteristics, and those who do, have them in differing amounts. There is a great difference between a coach with a lot of competitiveness and a little playfulness and vice versa. While different combinations of these aptitudes are not better than one over another overall, some are better suited to different environments than others (which will be discussed throughout the book).

Maybe you are considering coaching because you enjoyed playing volleyball in high school and want to share that love with others. Maybe there is a lack of club opportunities in the area and your daughter wants to play, so you're considering starting a team up by yourself. Or maybe you've even been recruited into coaching, though you're not sure if it is something you can handle.

One thing is almost guaranteed in coaching youth or school volleyball: You will need to keep your day job. If you are able to dedicate weekday evenings and weekends for 3-5 months to a sport you love, then you are going to be just fine. If your job is inflexible or your family or school responsibilities don't allow you to be busy during those hours, you may have to reconsider coaching for now.

COACHING PHILOSOPHY

If you've looked into coaching at all, you know that a lot of resources will talk about "coaching philosophy." But what does that actually mean? Coaches at all levels talk about it, but it is hardly ever defined anywhere. This is both good and bad. The good part about this is that you can make your coaching philosophy whatever you want it to be. However, if you've never coached before, you might not have any idea on where to start.

Your coaching philosophy should be a product of past experiences which have shaped your understanding of the game, combined with your core values. This will give you a great starting point for defining your coaching philosophy.

A few broad topics to consider: do you value winning above all else? What about skill development? Having fun? Be honest with yourself! If you think winning is most important, this will have implications for what age and level of player you will want to coach for.

It doesn't stop there! This will also impact your team rules, playing time decisions, communication with parents, and practically every aspect of coaching you can think of.

Coaching philosophy is so important, you should take time now to reflect on your values before reading any further. This will help you gain more from this guide than if you were reading without any sort of philosophical foundation.

Make a list of all your coaches who you can remember. These do not have to be volleyball coaches! Once you have this list, take ten minutes to answer these questions.

Reflection:

1. Who was my favorite coach and why?
2. What did he/she do that made me respect them as a coach?
3. What did I learn from him/her?
4. Who was my least favorite coach and why?
5. What did he/she do that made me not like them as a coach?
6. What did I learn from him/her?
7. How was my favorite coach different from my least favorite?
8. What values did I exhibit as a player?
9. What values do I want to instill in my players?
10. What would make my season a success?

Now, insert the corresponding answers into this template:

<u>My Coaching Philosophy:</u>

> As a coach, I value <u>top value from #8</u> and <u>top value from # 9</u> from myself and my team. I will carry on the good example of <u>top reason from #2</u> to make sure <u>answer from #7</u>. This will lead to success for my team, which I choose to define as <u>answer from #10</u>.

While we didn't use all of your answers from your reflection, they were necessary to develop the answers we did use. It does no good to reflect on what you won't do, because you need to have a plan for what you will do.

WHAT LEVEL TO COACH

Now you know that coaching volleyball is right for you and you have a rough idea of what your coaching philosophy is, the next step is to determine which age level you want to coach. This could be determined by a few things: The age of your daughter (if you're going to coach her team), the openings at your club of choice, or a stubbornness which forces you to seek out positions at any organizations, as long as you get to coach a certain age. You may have a preference going into your first year of coaching, or you may not. Let's review the possibilities.

Before diving into generalities, I think it's important to note that there can be significant differences between skill levels, amount of travel, and expected time commitments. If you are working at a high-resource (read: expensive) club, expect more of everything. More tournaments, more practices, longer hours, a longer season, higher skill levels, and more parent/family involvement. You will also have more pressure to perform well and the focus of the club, more often than not, will be to win.

On the opposite end of this spectrum, there are the low-resource clubs. These may be new programs which are starting or programs who keep fees low to encourage participation by the community. While there will still be

expectations to perform well and win, there will also be an emphasis on fun and general fitness. You may practice less often or for shorter

CHAPTER 1: DECIDING TO COACH

periods of time, and your season will almost certainly be shorter.

Regardless of age group, high and low-resource clubs will likely exhibit the traits discussed above. Keep in mind, the older the team, the higher the expectations will be.

Let's say that the club you are choosing to work for is a very average club. They are not in the top bracket, but outperform several teams in your region as well. Here's an overview of what you can expect.

12 and Under:

> This is likely their first exposure to volleyball. You must have a high level of patience for this group, as you will be teaching fundamentals over and over again and may not be getting much more advanced than learning how to get into base and what to do for a freeball. Positions can be taught at this level (and I encourage you to do so, no matter how difficult it is), but some programs may not choose to teach this yet.

14 and Under:

Over half of your team will have likely played volleyball before, and they should have a basic understanding of the foundational skills. Blocking may be a new concept to them, and learning how to play a position could be one of the things this group struggles with initially. However, stick it out and you can move on to some more advanced aspects of volleyball such as plays and adjusting to different offensive and defensive systems.

16 and Under:

Most of the girls on your team will be fairly serious about volleyball at this level. You may still have a few who will not continue on to 18 and under, but the chances of that are fairly slim. For this reason, among others, you can expect the level of play to be much higher even for a middle-of-the-pack team. This level will consist of critiquing technique and building mental toughness to overcome an opponent. Strength and agility training should also be implemented at this point,

CHAPTER 1: DECIDING TO COACH

if it hasn't been already.

<u>18 and Under:</u>

> Everyone playing 18 and under is trying to get a scholarship to play volleyball in college. Even teams closer to the bottom may still have one or two studs who are working on this goal, so if this is the level you are going to be coaching, make sure you can contribute at that level. If you haven't played at the college level or even on an 18 and under club team, I would suggest working your way into this age bracket as an assistant coach. Much more will be expected out of you in terms of technical knowledge, so make sure you are able to coach at a higher level before taking over an 18 and under team.

Coaching at a middle school or high school can be a similar experience but tends to be less competitive for most schools, largely due to the length of the season and also because of geographical restrictions on players. When you are able to travel 45 minutes to play for an elite club, you will do so if your skill level is a match.

However, during the school's season, you may be the only player in your district at that level and the playing field will level out a bit. Here is a breakdown of what you can expect to encounter as the coach of different levels of school ball.

Middle School:

> While 7th- and 8th-grade teams can vary in skill level, you can still expect to teach relatively the same skills. You will be covering very basic skills and techniques, but this should not be viewed as simple or only for poorly skilled coaches. Coaches at this level are setting the foundation for their players, and it is important that coaches at this level have a solid grasp of proper form and a positive mentality. The season is short, so expect things to click mid to late-season.

9th Grade:

> This level of coaching can be a toss-up, as the level of play likely depends on the availability and affordability of club teams in the area. With more club teams, you

CHAPTER 1: DECIDING TO COACH

are likely to have more advanced freshmen, and with fewer teams, you will likely have less skilled players. Your season is still short, but you are expected to prepare your players to move up to the junior varsity (JV) level by next year. This means correcting any mistakes on form, and incorporating strategies and plays the varsity team uses.

JV:

Assuming your high school has three levels, your next level up for coaching is at the JV level. This level has a lot to do with mental strategies, as you will have players who wanted to make varsity and didn't, and freshmen who got bumped up over their friends. Bringing the team together can be a huge challenge at this point in their volleyball careers. You should be running systems the same as varsity, though not with as much precision yet as the more skilled players. You need to understand what the varsity coach wants and create it.

Varsity:

> Similar to 18 and under, this group may have a few athletes interested and capable of playing at the next level. You will need to not only have the skill set and experience to run this team, but the entire program as well. Coaching at this level requires great foresight and an understanding of the game and inner workings of volleyball programs, as you will be in charge of most of the administrative tasks for your program as well. While you are still working on building skills to prepare them for the opportunity to play in college, you might also focus strictly on running your systems perfectly.

To summarize, you can never be 100% sure what you're getting into until tryouts are over and you know what girls you are working with. There are plenty of high school JV teams who play at a level similar to varsity at another school, and 16 and under club teams who could get beaten by an elite 14 and under team any day of the week.

CHAPTER 1: DECIDING TO COACH

If you plan far enough ahead, try to make it to a game or two the year before you start coaching and get an idea of what group of girls you would be able to properly coach the following year. Since this is not always possible, you'll have to speak with a variety of assistant and head coaches and administrators to get a clear idea in your head.

WHICH POSITION: HEAD OR ASSISTANT COACH

You probably have an idea of whether or not you want to be a head coach or assistant coach already. A lot of this will have to do with confidence in coaching ability, experience, and just natural disposition. If you find yourself comfortable leading groups or teams at work, or if you were a captain of a team before and are comfortable in a leadership position, being a head coach may be right for you. Alternatively, if you are most comfortable carrying out tasks (instead of creating them), you may be better suited to assistant coach.

Before you commit to a certain position, let's review common tasks and duties expected of both positions:

Head Coach:

- Leads the team
- Makes game-time decisions
- Plans and runs practice
- Schedules tournaments
- Responsible for skill development of entire team
- Communicates with parents and program director
- First responder for emergencies
- Delegates tasks to the assistant coach(es)
- May play as an extra in drills
- May keep stats
- Must understand all skills and be able to teach them

CHAPTER 1: DECIDING TO COACH

Assistant Coach:

- Completes tasks assigned by the head coach
- Runs drills while the head coach critiques
- Suggests rotations and line-ups
- Keeps stats for the team
- May play as an extra in drills
- First responder for emergencies
- Often responsible for paperwork
- May serve as position-specific coach

It is a common viewpoint in our society today that positions of leadership are what everyone should strive for. While this is true for some of the population, not everyone is comfortable in this role. So why do we push everyone into thinking the head coach is the ultimate position for all coaches? This overlooks the impact a great assistant can have on a team.

Additionally, if you want to ultimately coach a higher level team, it is best to start as an assistant at that level rather than serving as a head coach at a lower level and hoping to move up. You will already be proven at a certain level, and if your program was successful you will have plenty of opportunities to go elsewhere in years two or three and be the head coach.

WHERE TO COACH

If you live in a small town or a less populated area, you may only have one or two options on where to coach, those options being the high school or middle school. But if you live in a bigger city or metropolitan area where you have multiple clubs and countless high schools and middle schools within a 10-mile radius, you're going to need to make some decisions.

Start by researching all of the clubs in your area. Check out their websites at first, as this will give you an idea of how big they are. This might also point to how much you could get paid to coach there, but it's not a guarantee.

Another thing to consider is the opportunity to move up. What level can you see yourself

CHAPTER 1: DECIDING TO COACH

ultimately coaching? Not everyone starts out as a varsity coach at a high school, and maybe that isn't even an option for you. But if you can get your foot in the door as the coach of the freshman team, you'll become familiar with the program and make connections which might help you get to your dream position in the future. If the head coach isn't going anywhere anytime soon, they may still be a good reference for you and help you get interviews for other head coaching jobs in the area. If you had started coaching at the 7th-grade level, however, it would have been harder to earn the credibility to coach at the level you truly want.

Anytime you start a new job, you also want to consider the environment you'll be working in. Maybe you want to join a program that is accustomed to winning and want to be surrounded by other coaches and administrators with that attitude. A quick internet search will return results from years past, and the programs who repeatedly are in the top of their league or bracket would be good places to start looking for jobs.

Maybe you have more of the "builder" mentality. You want to go to a school and make a difference, taking a program which has struggled in the past and invest in the girls for a few years to turn the school around. Go back to your internet searches and look for programs near the bottom. While you may be able to turn a program around in one season, expect this transformation to take at least two or three years. You will also need to instill a new culture into the program, and that takes a while to get buy-in from players, parents, supporters, and administration.

GETTING YOUR FOOT IN THE DOOR

As with any job, getting your first opportunity is all about who you know. A great place to begin your job search is through your former coaches or athletic directors if you plan on staying close to home. Head coach positions are easier to come by in middle schools and high schools if you are also licensed to teach, but this is often not required for assistant coaches.

Reach out to your former coaches through a quick phone call or email, or better yet, swing by to watch a game and speak with them briefly afterward. While this approach takes a little forethought, it will certainly seem sincere and

CHAPTER 1: DECIDING TO COACH

will give you an easy icebreaker (fingers crossed that the team wins). Congratulate them on a game well played, and when they ask you how you are doing or what you've been up to, indicate your interest in pursuing coaching.

If this is during their season, they likely do not need any more coaches, though they may ask if you want to swing by and volunteer sometime. They may also direct you to individuals associated with the local club team. Either response is going to open a door for you, so be prepared to take them up on the offer on the spot if you truly are interested in coaching and it's for a position you are looking for.

Another way to discover open positions is to call up the club director for clubs in the local area. This works well if you have relocated and live in a new town with fairly limited connections. They will often be able to tell you any job openings or might direct you towards some of their returning head coaches who may be looking for assistant coaches. If there's one thing to keep in mind, it's that coaches are mobile, so jobs are always opening up.

Finally, working for local fitness clubs or park

districts may lead to coaching opportunities. If you are able to demonstrate that you can lead an eight-week program for 5th and 6th graders, you will likely make connections in the area which lead to referrals or at least connections to reach out to in the local volleyball network. Even reffing adult volleyball leagues will put you in touch with people who know someone that coaches volleyball!

EXPECTATIONS

I think this is important to discuss in the closing section of this chapter the topic of expectations. Going in, you should have low expectations. To be clear, I am not advocating low expectations in the sense that I don't want you to get your hopes up about your first season, because it might turn out not to be everything you're hoping for. Just the opposite. I want you to be excited! I want you to have high hopes! And I want you to know the realities you'll likely face.

Let's address (in my mind) the elephant in the room. You will likely not be compensated at a level that you'd prefer. My first coaching job, I was getting a stipend of $300 a month. My assistant wasn't getting anything, so I split down

CHAPTER 1: DECIDING TO COACH

the middle with her (show appreciation for your assistants)! I was almost able to pay for gas. But I loved coaching, and so did my assistant. Coaching was essentially a hobby rather than a source of income.

It can go higher (much higher, depending on the level you're coaching at), but if you are just starting out, expect to make what a volunteer would make (aka, nothing), or earn up to $1,000 a month if you're in a high school or middle school setting. The "elephant in the room" saying is appropriate, as you'll be earning peanuts (and coaching can feel like you're in a circus).

Maybe you're already aware of this, and are coaching simply because you want to share your joy of volleyball, or perhaps your daughter is going to play and you want to coach her. Money may not be your main concern. Let's address the "sharing the love of volleyball" perspective.

Expectation: everyone will love volleyball and want to get better and will have fun at every practice. Reality: one or two girls on the team are playing because their parents are making them, or because their friends play so they figured they'd try it out. A few more will start basketball in the middle of your season (if it's club) and will be more excited about basketball than they will be about volleyball. This can be a big letdown when you realize that not everyone is having as much fun as you are.

Or if you're coaching your daughter, maybe your intention was to provide a good environment for her to grow and play a sport she loves, and spend time with her in the process. But what if she's not the best player? What if you get in fights on the drive home from practice because she thinks that other girls get more playing time than her?

Overall, my warning to you is this. Whatever hopes and expectations you have going into the season, remember that you need to temper them with reality. You CAN make money coaching, you CAN have a great season where all of your players love volleyball, and you CAN build a great relationship with your daughter by coaching her team.

Know why you're getting into coaching, but don't daydream about how wonderful it's going to be. Plan ahead and know what your personal goals are, but don't get stuck wishing things would turn out how you imagined. Keep your expectations low, and you will experience happiness after your season surpasses them.

COACHING VOLLEYBALL

CHAPTER 2: PRESEASON PREPARATION

So you've found the perfect place for you to coach! You decided what level to coach, which club or school offered you the opportunities you're looking for, and most importantly, have created a coaching philosophy which gets you excited to step onto the court for the first time.

Before you even begin working with your team, you need to take a few steps to set yourself up for success during your first season.

MEET YOUR NEW BOSS

Depending on which position you scored, you'll want to meet with your boss to discuss expectations for the season and get your planning underway, if you haven't already. If you are a head coach, you'll want to meet with your club director or athletic director, as this is who will need to have your back if parents start to voice opinions on your coaching style (it'll be playing time nine times out of ten).

Getting to know your administrator works to your advantage, as you will both leave this meeting with expectations for the season moving forward. You can also leave on a good note, so if anything does come up, you'll be able to contact them right away with no worries.

Meeting this person is more about formality and building a bond which you can rely on for support. You do not need to discuss more than your coaching philosophy, as administrators tend to stay out of the day-to-day operations. Their job is to make sure all the logistics are taken care of for you to succeed.

If you are an assistant coach, go for coffee or lunch with your head coach and get to know each other, if you don't already. This meeting is a great time to discuss coaching philosophy and how that will translate into your actual season.

Which types of defense are you familiar with? What level of play are you expecting your team to be able to compete at? Are there advanced

CHAPTER 2: PRESEASON PREPARATION

<u>skills you'd like to teach your team</u>, or are you interested in reinforcing the basics?

Use the coaching philosophy reflection from chapter one as a guide to understanding the coaching philosophy of your head coach, if they are not able to articulate it to you. Sharing this with each other helps layout the foundation which your team will be built upon, and also help in determining roles.

The roles of head coaches and assistant coaches discussed in chapter one gave you a good idea of the typical responsibilities you'd have in either position, but your head coach may have other thoughts on responsibilities. Maybe you'll be responsible for lineups, and they prefer to be the down-ref during tournaments. *My role & responsibilities*

Clarify your role before the season starts and <u>know which responsibilities are most important</u>. Make sure you take a notebook with you when you go to this meeting so you can keep track of all of your good ideas.

By the end of your meeting, you should have a chart similar to the one which follows with your top five responsibilities written down and the importance which they hold for the head coach.

This will help you prioritize throughout the season.

Creating a list of your top five responsibilities for the season helps assistants know how they can best help the head coach.

RESPONSIBILITIES	RANK
Coach setters during practice	2
Responsible for warm-up drill every practice	1
Create write-ups for local newspapers	4
Create reffing schedule for tournaments	5
Keep stats during games	3

After this meeting you'll probably want to run home and come up with as many warm-up drills as you can! Isn't this fun!? You'll notice coaching is a lot more about making sure the team functions rather than just practicing and coaching during games. A lot of the work is administrative in nature. Which leads me to my next point…

CHAPTER 2: PRESEASON PREPARATION

PAPERWORK, PAPERWORK, PAPERWORK

You've got a lot to do before the season starts. A LOT. For starters, you will have to pass a background check and get fingerprinted since you will be working with children. You should also have your CPR/AED/First Aid certifications if you do not already. These are just the beginning.

You will probably need to complete a number of school-specific trainings if you are coaching for a high school or middle school. The same goes for the association in which you are coaching. The organizations might be kind and bundle the information together, but expect to bounce around between online trainings and in-person sessions to complete everything. Work on these as early as possible, because you often are not allowed to coach without having completed the trainings.

You may have to seek out referee training as well, typically only when coaching club volleyball. Volleyball is a strange sport in which you are expected to referee at tournaments. Not just you, but your team as well. So before you try to get ahead of the game and do all your training before checking in with your boss, wait on the referee training. Your players will have to go to the training as well, so you might as well all go together.

The paperwork should end at this point, right? You'll have easily spent around five hours (if not more) getting the above-mentioned completed and turned in. Don't forget, there are also employment forms you need to complete such as tax forms before you begin. The form you fill out may vary from institution to institution, as some coaches are considered employees, while others are hired as independent contractors. I don't do taxes, so I suggest you speak with someone who does. This way you will understand what your type of classification means for you come April.

Hopefully, you are done with preseason paperwork at this point and can put the boring stuff behind you. Your school or club may have additional requirements though, so before you even consider stepping on the court, check with your higher-ups. An athletic director or club director should give you your final clearance (preferably in email so it's in writing) before you start work as a coach.

To recap:

- Background check
- CPR/AED/First Aid certifications
- School-specific training & certifications
- Association specific training
- Referee training
- Tax paperwork
- Miscellaneous

There are a lot of forms and training sessions you will need to complete, so once you know what they are, start chipping away at them. Unfortunately, there can be costs associated with a few of the trainings as well. I have not had a school or club pay for most of these in the past, but you may be at a school with more resources who takes care of the expenses for you. While having to pay for concussion training can be a bummer, you're almost to the fun stuff!

BUY EQUIPMENT

You're just about ready to get on the court for this first time! But are you ready? Realizing mid-tryout or mid-practice that you forgot an essential piece of equipment can range from mild annoyance to major panic.

No stopwatch during practice? Get your phone out and use the timer. No whistle when you step onto the ref stand? You'll have to hunt someone down and hope they have an extra one, forcing both teams to wait for your return.

While you may enjoy multiple trips to the store, I don't. Knowing what you'll need throughout the season can make one trip to the store or one online shopping session be all you need.

Here is a list of items to buy before you even begin tryouts to make sure you get off to a smooth start and ready for the season:

Necessary:

- Whistle with lanyard
- Backpack
- Binder

CHAPTER 2: PRESEASON PREPARATION

- Pens
- Pencils
- Notebooks
- Wristwatch with a stopwatch feature

Optional:

- First aid kit
- New shoes
- Practice gear

Let's address the first aid kit first. Is it really optional? No. You need to have one. It's listed as optional because most clubs and schools will provide their coaches with a first aid kit before the season even begins, and it will need to be at every practice, match, and tournament.

If they don't give you one? Ask for one first, because you really shouldn't be the one footing this bill. If for some reason you don't get one or don't think the supplies are adequate, buy your own. I usually bring a few extra icepacks, since volleyball players are notorious for ankle injuries.

On a less serious note, while shoes appropriate for jumping into practice at any second are a definite must-have, most people will already have a pair of tennis shoes which will work just fine. But I will tell you, it gets you excited and pumped to start a new season to step out onto the court with new purple shoes and all black workout gear when those are your team's colors.

Showing up to a tournament in blue shoes when your team is yellow isn't necessarily the worst thing ever, but having the same color of yellow, black, or grey shoes would make the team look more unified.

CHAPTER 3: TRYOUTS

Tryouts are an exciting time of the year for both coaches and players. Stepping into the gym, you will be so filled with excitement at the potential you see all around you. Follow these tips to make sure your tryouts run smoothly and that you are testing players for skills which will actually help you determine their playing ability.

SETUP

Depending on whether or not you are joining an existing club or if you have decided to take the plunge and start your own team, knowing a few key logistical components for tryouts will help the process run smoother and will reduce your day-of anxiety.

For starters, make sure you have gym space secured. Many schools will close over the summer for work on their floors, so knowing when this will be over and the gym will be available is important. Arranging a time is also important, since many of your players will unlikely be able to drive themselves to tryouts. A 10:00am start time may work for you, but what about the family that works and is unable to find a ride for their daughter?

Marketing for tryouts should consist of at least a newspaper ad every week starting a month out, if not more. If you are coaching at a school, it should be posted on the school's reader board. You can also increase reach if you market through social media accounts. These are free to setup and allow you access to the parents of potential players. Parents are great at sharing this message. If there are any questions, a direct message or post will clear up any confusion.

Once your marketing is out, you will need to create a schedule for your tryouts, and determine how teams will be announced. You should also go into tryouts with an idea of how many players you can handle on a team (9-10 is usually good for all ages). This number will

CHAPTER 3: TRYOUTS

depend on the level of your club and your philosophy on coaching, and where a clear distinction is after your tryout results are in.

When the day finally arrives, you will also need to know who is going to:

- Bring all of the supplies and equipment
- Setup the courts
- Pump up balls
- Collect money (if charging a fee)
- Collect and verify paperwork is complete
- Run the drills
- Who is scoring
- How will scoring be done

If you do not have tryouts meticulously planned out, you run the risk of appearing unorganized and inexperienced. As a first year coach, you want to avoid this at all costs! Those who are helping you may chuckle that you have the day planned down to the minute, but it will impress the families of the girls trying out.

SKILLS TO TEST FOR

Our skills & rubric for tryouts

For volleyball, there are a few givens when it comes to skills you need to test for. Some of these skills are considered "hard" skills, as in you can determine through numbers whether or not a person has these skills. These hard skills are:

- Passing
- Setting
- Attacking
- Serving

Coaches will often have ratings for "soft" skills, or more intangible characteristics which you get a feeling for rather than can measure.

These soft skills can include:

- Coachability
- Teamwork
- Leadership
- Hustle
- Communication

While hard skills will have straight forward scores to determine skill level, the soft skills are more subjective and based on intuition or gut feelings. Scores for players on soft skills will likely vary by coach, because your perception of hustling is probably different than mine. These soft skills can be used as a tie-breaker if there are any tough decisions to make as to where to cut off your roster.

There are also more hard skills which are more focused on athleticism in general rather than playing ability. These skills are discussed more in the following section.

TESTING DESIGNS

Unless your first year coaching involves the first year that a program is in existence, you will probably help run tryouts which are already established. Even if you are taking over a middle school program, there will probably be tryout sheets which were used in the past and will be used moving forward.

If you're starting your own program, or have decided you want to make an existing program your own, keep a few things in mind when determining what to test for and how to test.

Tryouts are typically broken down into three segments:

- Athletic ability testing
- Individual volleyball skills
- Team volleyball skills

By testing players in these different situations, you get a better idea of how they will function as teammate, as an individual, and as a leader.

Athletic ability testing:

Athletic ability testing is typically done through push-ups, sit-ups, sprints, and other necessary skills which are important to volleyball, but are not technically volleyball skills.

When you are creating or reviewing this portion of your tryouts, make sure to ask yourself these two questions:

- Is this actually relevant to volleyball?
- Do I consider this important for my players?

I have been a part of team tryouts as a coach

where certain skills were tested, but were not considered tie-breakers when trying to place players on teams. Why make them stress out and do a 40-yard dash if it doesn't even matter, right? Is there ever a point in their volleyball career where sprinting 40 yards will actually be a part of the game? Unlikely.

I have included a cheat sheet for you of a few skills to test for, in alphabetical order, along with their applicability to the game.

ATHLETIC ABILITY TEST	APPLICABILITY
*Push-ups	Upper body strength
Shuffle drills	Side-to-side movement
*Sit-ups	Core strength
Star-Drill	Ability to change direction quickly
Vertical: 3-step approach	Height of attack
Vertical: block jump	Height of block

By testing athletic ability, you can understand the athleticism of your players. This is especially beneficial when coaching younger players who may not have developed their volleyball skills yet.

Why the asterisks next to push-ups and sit-ups? These skills may or may not be useful for you. They are very common in tryouts, yet hold very little merit in the sport of volleyball. Yes, they do show upper body and core strength. But these can also be shown through the power of their attacks.

Still, I recommend using these tests if you are coaching young players who may not be able to successfully perform volleyball skills, but can pump out 50 pushups in three minutes at 12 years old. Those are the kids you want on your team; you'll just need to teach them to harness that power.

Scoring for athletic ability tests should assign a score for performance based on a range of repetitions, times, heights, etc. Here is an example of scoring for consecutive pushups:

PUSHUPS	SCORE
0-20	0
20-30	2
30-40	4
40-50	6
50-60	8
60+	10

By setting a range ahead of time with the scoring already in place, you can keep your

reviews of players as objective as possible.

Create additional charts such as this and post them at different stations or hand them out to all tryout participants. Notice that I said "consecutive" pushups. This means no dropping a knee between. If you have rules such as this, tell the girls at the beginning of tryouts and remind them often. Any reason to allege unfair tryout conditions can a source of contention with families after teams are decided.

When creating charts for the shuffle drill and star drill you will want to use time as measurement. For testing the approach and block jump, track both vertical (the difference between standing height reached and top height touched after jumping) and the highest point reached. You may have someone with a 30" vertical, but if she is only 5'2" she probably won't reach as high as your 6'2" player.

Individual volleyball skills:

Next, we have individual volleyball skills. This is when you will test each player's ability to perform when skill at a time in a controlled environment. This will allow for fair and objective judging of skills.

The most common individual volleyball skills to test for are passing, setting, attacking, and serving. You can mix in others, but usually shuffling around to stations with a large group and measuring these skills will take some time.

Scoring can be completed by considering accuracy, power, and technique. There are many examples of tryout scoring in these areas for free online if you need to build from scratch.

CHAPTER 3: TRYOUTS

<u>Team volleyball skills:</u> *[handwritten: Who is evaluating?]*

Finally, <u>most tryouts will conclude with some form of scrimmage</u>. It may be a round-robin event, queen of the court, or some other game-like drill. These drills show off most of the individual skills which were tested for, except in a game-like setting.

It's best if this portion of tryouts is administered by assistant coaches or volunteers who will not be making decisions on team assignments.

This time will allow evaluating coaches to preliminarily assess players and see where most of them fall in terms of scoring and ranking. Then, while the scrimmaging is still going on, they are able to more closely watch in-between players. These are the players who may either make the varsity team or the JV team (or JV versus freshman team, etc.).

Coaches may also make <u>additional observations at this time on characteristics such as leadership or teamwork</u>. This is a crucial time for coaches to actively observe all players, because there may be certain characteristics which show at this time that are more (or less) desirable than what the athletic and individual volleyball skill scores show.

Having a place to make notes on certain players is important at this time so that you can add observations to their score sheets later, if they have not already been collected.

The final whistle will blow, and you or another authority figure at the tryout will need to give a small speech thanking everyone for attending. Details on announcements should be given, along with one final thank you before dismissing the tryout participants.

Now comes the hard part.

MAKING DECISIONS

This will be your first real test when it comes to decision making as a coach. And not to put pressure on you, but this is a pretty big decision. So let's discuss a few things which you should consider before making your final roster.

First, the younger the player, the more likely that their natural athletic ability will impact their ability to play. As discussed previously, this is when push-ups and sit-ups might actually be beneficial as a part of your evaluation criteria.

You will also want to watch them during the scrimmage portion to see how they interact with others and if they are coachable.

On the flipside, if you have a 12-year-old who already has her three-step approach down and has played for two years but couldn't do a push-up for anything? Just let it go. Volleyball skills triumph in this scenario.

If your team is older, more emphasis should be placed on volleyball skills. Differentiation between middle blockers or setters can be seen more clearly through the individual portion than during team-play, so if you know ahead of time that there will be a battle for a certain position, be sure to pay close attention during individual skill tests.

This leads to another idea which you should keep in mind during tryouts: Positions. You may have three girls dominate the setting portion of tryouts, but how many setters can one team handle?

My opinion? No more than two, and at least one should be able to function as a front row player as well. So what do you do here? Do you take on the third setter because of her high overall score and have her sit the bench? Do you put her on the JV team and have her function as a great leader there? Could you keep her on varsity and just make her an outside hitter instead?

This is one area where I will not try to answer the question for you. There are pros and cons to each scenario. Hypothetically, if she sits the bench with you, she doesn't develop her skills, loses confidence, and doesn't work hard to reach team goals.

Depending on her attitude, however, she could very well be the exact opposite of that statement. Maybe she does develop her skill. Maybe she works harder than your other setters and becomes a starter midway through the season. She could even contribute more than anyone on the team to the goals you originally set for them.

When you have decisions like this to make, they will never be easy and no answer will ever feel right. Refer back to your coaching philosophy and see how this player might fit into that puzzle. Do what is going to move your team towards your definition of success. This is all you can do in this situation.

ANNOUNCING YOUR TEAM

The jitters that players will feel leading up to tryouts can pale in comparison to the nervousness and anxiety which can set in after all is said and done and they are waiting to hear back from the coaches.

Before tryouts begin, you will need to decide how you will announce teams. I have coached for organizations which decided for me that coaches would announce teams at the end of tryouts, or that I must post tryout results two hours after the event on the door to the facility for players to come and check. As a player, one of my teams actually mailed out team placements after two agonizing weeks, and other years I was personally called by coaches.

Needless to say, there are a lot of ways to announce your team. Each way will have pros and cons, so if you are able to determine or influence how your team will be announced, take the following advantages and disadvantages into consideration:

<u>Window of time:</u>

> Announcing teams right after tryouts was difficult. There was very little time for deliberation. While the final portions of tryouts were taken into consideration, in the back of our minds we were focusing on creating teams a little more than we should have been. We also were starting practice right away and needed teams to

be made. If you have a while before your season begins, give yourself more time.

Competitiveness:

If you are coaching at an elite club or school, give yourself the appropriate amount of time to consider alternative options. You will likely have many girls who are qualified to be on your team, so let yourself entertain the different options for a day or two before you make your decision. Alternatively, if there is little competition to make the team, you can go a little easier on yourself. You're still trying to make the best decision for your team moving forward, but the process should not last as long.

Formality:

I think this equates to prestige of the club or team you are coaching for. If the program is expensive and the performance is at an elite level, you want there to be a little more grandeur associated with the team. If your team has modest performance every year, it might be a little over the top to mail out a formal letter to each player on your team.

Regardless of what has been done in the past to announce teams, keep in mind that how you make the announcement will build the foundation of your culture. Want to run a team with more formality? Mail out or call players who make the team. You're building a brand for your team, so keep in mind that tryouts have an early impact on that brand.

Announcing the team is only the beginning. You may get responses to your announcement.

Remember that player who you weren't sure if they should be on the top team or the next team down? Well, let's imagine for a second that you placed them on the JV team. You're probably going to have some angry parents.

Make sure you've discussed this with your club or athletic director, since they'll probably get the first angry phone call. They may want you to handle it by calling and discussing the matter with the family, or they may stand behind your decision and refuse to discuss the matter.

Either way, know what your boss's response will be so that you can present an organized and unified front to any questioning. Assuming you made your decisions on objective criteria presented at tryouts, you should have full faith in your team assignments.

COACHING VOLLEYBALL

CHAPTER 4: BEGINNING OF THE SEASON

You may be thinking, "finally, we get to practice!" The answer is yes and no. Of course, you get to practice once the season starts, but there are still a few administrative tasks which need to be completed. There is more to this coaching stuff than just running practice and playing games. Although you will undoubtedly be ready to jump right in, there are a few more tasks you need to take care of before you begin to actually start coaching.

The beginning of the season has a lot of formalities which need to take place, including meeting with the families of your team and setting expectations, establishing team rules, ordering uniforms, and more.

On the bright side, you actually get to start practice, which is why you were drawn to coaching in the first place, right?

MEETING THE PARENTS

Meeting the parents can be an intimidating situation. Unless you are from a small town where everyone knows everyone, you'll be going into this meeting with no idea what personalities you'll encounter.

From the get-go, everyone will be extremely friendly. Most of them will be just as excited as you are about the upcoming season and will be eager to hear your plans for the team.

However, this doesn't mean you can go into the meeting totally relaxed and without preparation. Families will have questions for you, and the ones who will ask questions are the ones who are not concerned with sugar-coating their inquiries.

This is why you try to address many of these topics in a welcome speech/presentation, so you give off the vibe of being prepared and that you are fully capable of leading their daughters.

CHAPTER 4: BEGINNING OF THE SEASON

Here are some examples of the questions you might be asked at your first meeting of the year:

- How long have you been coaching?
- Did you play?
- How much traveling are we going to do?
- How do you decide playing time?
- What uniforms are we getting?
- Can you give my daughter a ride?
- When are practices going to be?
- How do you think we'll do this year?

Try to address as many of these questions as you can in your introduction to the team. The fewer questions there are, the quicker everyone will get out of the meeting, which busy parents appreciate.

Additionally, if you answer some of these questions upfront, like "How long have you been coaching," it will feel less like you're hiding things and you will seem much more confident and trustworthy.

Do your research, have your ducks in a row, and lay it all out on the table.

A sample introduction for a first-year coach could sound like this:

> "Hello everyone, my name is Whitney Bartiuk and this is my first year coaching volleyball. Although I am new to coaching, I started playing volleyball when I was in 6th grade and have been playing ever since. While in high school I worked at every summer camp and even led camp my senior year.
>
> What I loved about coaching during camp was seeing the girls develop their skills and watching their enthusiasm for the game grow.
>
> Although it's my first year coaching, I know that this program has been very successful in the past. I plan to build on those successes with an aggressive playing style which still develops the entire team."

You should then go over team rules (detailed in subsequent sections), established travel plans, the possibility for any additional travel, uniform ordering (if not already in place), practice schedules, and team policies.

Once your presentation is done, open the floor for questions. You should have addressed most of the topics which apply to everyone, so you may get individual questions at this point. Note that you can discuss individual questions afterward so the group can be dismissed.

If you do not already have it, have sheets which families can complete and pass around at the meeting for contact information. Follow the meeting up with an email summarizing your points and reiterating any questions which you answered during the meeting.

One final note. Although I often refer to family members as "parents" throughout these pages, please be aware that sometimes you may be communicating with aunts, uncles, grandparents, legal guardians, stepparents, cousins… the list goes on and on.

I recommend being inclusive in your speech because not everyone will have a "mom and dad" as their primary support system. I prefer to use the term "family" as often as possible since this has always captured everyone who is a legal guardian for my girls.

So despite my use of the term "parents" on occasion, please know the family structure for your players before you say anything which excludes someone who cares for one of your girls.

MORE PAPERWORK

I know, I know, you thought you were done with paperwork. But I have good news for you. This is FUN paperwork! Really. Before the season started you had to get all of your employment forms and certifications done. Now that you have your team chosen, there are a few more "paperwork" tasks which you should do. This is a time when you can be creative, so embrace the fun that comes along with coaching. If you're not the creative type, however, you can also choose to find some of these items online and save yourself the time.

Regardless of your coaching philosophy, you'll need to be clear about at least one topic during the season: team rules. While discipline is discussed a little later on, discipline should only happen after team rules are broken.

CHAPTER 4: BEGINNING OF THE SEASON

After reading the Discipline section, create a list of your team rules and print out enough to give to each player and also to distribute to families at your first meeting together. This way everyone knows what is expected of them and is not caught off guard when you take disciplinary action. If you have different levels or kinds of discipline depending on the rule which was broken, list that out as well. Not only will this help deter rule breaking, but it will also help you stay consistent.

Once you've created your team rules, you need to hand them out to your players. While you could just give the paper to each girl and hope she at least keeps it somewhere in her gym bag, I prefer to hand out team rules in a folder which I customize for each player. This could be as simple as writing their name and number in the top right-hand corner.

You could get a little more crafty if that's what you're into, and add stickers, quotes, drawings, etc. on their folder. It might also be fun to have a folder decorating station at the beginning of the year meeting to keep the players entertained while you talk to the families. Younger players will probably appreciate this more, but the right group of high schoolers might enjoy it just as much.

So why hand out folders when all you're doing is handing out team rules? A folder is generally more sturdy than the paper, which will likely end up crumpled at the bottom of their bag next to a rogue sock which they're not even sure is theirs. But now you have a safe place for other papers to go if needed. Say you're traveling for a tournament and want to hand out the information at practice. It will be safe in the folder. Maybe you want to create a habit of writing down team and personal goals before each match. That can go in the folder too. You're helping yourself in the long run by giving them a safe place to store anything you think is important enough to print out and give to them.

Later on in this book, we'll look at keeping stats for your team. In that chapter I will give you tons of reasons to implement stat tracking in the beginning of your season, but I want to give you a tool now which will help you use stats for each individual on your team, not just at the broad level.

CHAPTER 4: BEGINNING OF THE SEASON

If you search hard enough online, you can download a personal stat tracker for your players. This encourages one-on-one discussions with your players if you have the time, but can also be an easy way to communicate about their individual performance and growth without having to use practice time to have these meetings.

If you'd prefer to create your own personal stat tracker, consider including the following spaces to communicate growth over the season:

- Serving percentage
- Passing percentage
- Setting percentage
- Attacking percentage
- Blocks, kills, aces, assists, digs
- Notes

To demonstrate growth, I like to show the team an average percentage, not including the most recent match or tournament. Then I have a column with the same stats, but for only the most recent match or tournament. This will show the players how their most recent performance stacks up against their previous performance.

During my second year of coaching, I also included the team percentages so they could see where they were in relation to everyone else on the team. I decided to take this stat off of the form itself and instead share these numbers verbally. Team stats are a good measure which you should definitely track, but you are adding insult to injury when someone realizes they're dragging down the team passing percentage every tournament. They'll know when you announce team stats, there's no reason to include it on their personal stat tracker.

If you're going to have meetings after every competition to discuss individual progress, you can give players one sheet which they can use all year to track their stats. If you'd prefer to hand out stats and only have meetings when necessary, I recommend just handing out a new sheet after every match or tournament.

One word of caution on personal stat trackers. Your players can take these very literally and the self-confidence of younger players especially may suffer. Communicate with your team that they are a learning tool and cannot capture everything which a player brings to the team. Enthusiasm and teamwork are just as important, but those are hard to measure. Add positive comments in the Notes section to discuss ways in which a player contributed that is not made obvious by the stats.

BUILDING TRUST AND CULTURE

Remember in the very beginning when I said that some parts of this book will have a greater impact on your season than others? Well, this is one of those areas. And it is major. Right behind your coaching philosophy is your ability to build a positive and productive team culture. And while coaching philosophy and culture are of the utmost importance, your influence will not extend as far as you hope without first building trust.

To start, let's talk about trust. We all know in our gut when we trust someone or not, but what behaviors actually generate trust?

Think back to your former coaches. Were you ever told, "You're going to get a lot of playing time today," only to sit the bench, like always? Or have you ever gone back to serve, only to see your coach panic and call for a substitution, even though they weren't sure who they were going to put in? Or have you ever asked your coach about playing a new position or trying a new play, been told yes, and then never get the opportunity?

These experiences likely deteriorated your trust in your coach and impacted your commitment to the team and their goals. While it occasionally happens, breaking promises to your players or not being prepared for certain situations on a regular basis is one of the quickest ways to fail as a leader of your team.

So how do you build and maintain trust? For starters, know your coaching philosophy. If you haven't taken the time yet, go back to Chapter 1 and do this NOW! This will show you your true "coaching personality." When you understand that, you can create policies around your values which you are more likely to follow, even during high-intensity and high-stress situations.

How do you do that? It's mostly self-monitoring. Want to brighten someone's day by

CHAPTER 4: BEGINNING OF THE SEASON

telling them that they're going to get more playing time? Just don't. Even if your intention is to get them in, don't tell them this a few hours before the match when you're still uncertain of all the playing conditions.

Do they need a heads up? Yes. But only when you know for sure that they're going in, not when you think it would be nice if you could get them more playing time.

Or if they want to try a new position and you think the time is right, let them know before a match so they can warm-up in that position. Don't think you'll get them in? Need them in their regular position? Just tell them that. Delivering bad or unwanted news is hard, but if your players know that you're being honest with them, the trust will build.

Some pointers:
- Don't overpromise
- If the answer is no, say no
- Explain decisions if the situation calls for an explanation

- Fight the urge to explain decisions otherwise
- Say what you mean
- Follow through with promises
- If you fail to meet a promise, sincerely apologize

Behind only your coaching philosophy and trust, building team culture is one of the foundations of the season which you need to make a priority. Your culture is essentially a mixture of the most dominant personalities on your team and your values.

In coaching volleyball, and girls especially, it is important to maintain a positive and supportive culture. This doesn't mean you have to start off each practice with a group hug or give constant praise, but the environment should encourage growth.

This can work for all coaching philosophies, whether you see yourself as more of a drill sergeant or a cheerleader.

Think about the behaviors and rituals you want to build into your culture. I'll share a few of my favorite experiences as a coach to get you

CHAPTER 4: BEGINNING OF THE SEASON

started. Start by focusing on the values you want to see in your players and the behaviors which would demonstrate those values. Then come up with a few reinforcements you'd like to use for each behavior. Here are some of my personal favorites.

VALUE	BEHAVIORS WANTED	REINFORCEMENT
Aggression	Hitting downballs, diving.	Verbal praise, celebrate passes, give stickers.
Bench Involvement	Bench cheering, ready to go in at all times, suggesting plays during matches.	Keeping stats, bench cheers, standing up.
Strategic Play	Play calling, captain-led huddles.	Ask team to call a play and run it, celebrate tips in open areas.

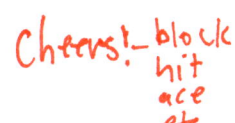

Cheers! - block, hit, ace, etc.

By understanding what you want out of your players, you are able to better communicate your expectations to them. Designing reinforcements ahead of time leaves only one task remaining: implementation.

Now try and come up with your own list! Bounce back and forth between your values and behaviors wanted, then think of how you'll reinforce them. Consistency is key here! Make sure the reinforcements are something you can keep up, otherwise the behaviors may not be consistent either.

You might find that, throughout the season, you will add new behaviors to your "wish list." And you'll probably change some of your reinforcements if they aren't working, and add new ones. Only change something if it absolutely does not work, or if you find that you cannot keep up with it.

For example, I place a high value on aggressiveness. During one of my years coaching club, I took Valentine's Day cards to my girls at a tournament on February 14th.

CHAPTER 4: BEGINNING OF THE SEASON

Since I only had ten girls, I brought along the extras with the intention of giving more out to siblings who were at the tournament.

I had a ton of leftover stickers from the packet, and halfway through the tournament one of my players pancaked a ball, which I absolutely love because it shows so much aggression and an implementation of skills we were working on in practice.

The other team called a timeout and as my team came rushing in, excited by the play, I told that girl she would get a heart sticker for such a great play! Everyone was excited and cheered more. And so began the ritual of giving out heart stickers for amazing plays.

My setter chasing down a shanked pass 20 feet behind the service line, a backrow player calling off a front row player to downball a bad set instead of letting it get passed over… These events happened often enough to keep the stickers in mind, yet were rare enough to be special, probably once or twice a tournament.

My players got excited about it. I was excited about it. It was easy to maintain and it reinforced the type of play I wanted. When someone would make a great play, there would usually be one or two girls yelling "heart sticker!" It was perfect.

Fast forward to the following season. A few of the same girls are on my team, and I am excited to use stickers as bribery for good play yet again. I announce this to the team at our first meeting, expecting the same excitement and enthusiasm which existed with my previous team.

However, this group of girls was older, and quite frankly, not even mildly enthused about stickers. Gotta love high schoolers. I was a little taken aback by their sideways glances and raised eyebrows, but just KNEW that once we started playing and they started earning their stickers, they would love it.

This was never the case. Try as I might, the stickers never stuck. I tried and tried, but it eventually proved to be more of a distraction than a source of unity. Halfway through the season I admitted defeat and ditched the stickers.

If anything, that experience taught me that I cannot force traditions onto a team, especially when they develop organically from a team made up of completely different individuals.

So when you are trying to create reinforcements of your preferred behaviors, just be aware that some may not work as you planned, and be ok with abandoning your efforts when you're positive they won't catch on or work for your team. Try things out that worked for you when you played, but realize that your team might not be as excited as you are.

Just because something doesn't catch on initially, doesn't mean it won't work. I enjoy mixing up teams and warm-up partners, but telling the girls to pick a new partner literally never works. And someone is always complaining. It's horrible.

I started asking my girls to line up alphabetically by their favorite color, favorite flavor of gum, favorite band, etc. Then I just separate them down the middle or count off by twos to split them up evenly. When I start this with my teams, they all look at me as if I am treating them like children.

Around the second or third week, they get more excited, and their answers get weirder as they become more comfortable with everyone. This reinforcement bonds them all and gives them things to talk about, and works towards my value of the team getting along. It is weird how much two girls can bond over both loving turquoise.

DISCIPLINE

You've already created rules and discussed them both with your players as well as their families. Everyone is on the same page. Let's say you have some pretty basic rules, like no kicking the ball, no swearing, no side conversations during huddles, etc.

So what happens when one of your girls *gasp* breaks one of these rules?

This is a major decision you need to make before the season begins, because the first time it happens, it sets a precedent. Are you going to let it slide? Will you give out warning after warning, yet do nothing about it in the end? Or will you stop everything and send your players to the service line and make them run until you think you get the point across? Drop in the middle of a match and do push-ups?

CHAPTER 4: BEGINNING OF THE SEASON

As a former player, we probably all experienced differing disciplinary styles coming from our coaches. Maybe even differences from the same coach, depending on their mood. The head coach may have been extremely strict while the assistant was mainly there to encourage the girls on your team.

While you don't come into your first season wondering what sort of punishment your team will serve for various offenses, it is something you need to decide on. Make sure your other coaches are on the same page.

Not sure where to start? Think about this. The whole point of discipline is to make your girls stop some sort of behavior. Usually one they know they shouldn't do, but decide to engage in anyway. The best punishment is one that they do not want, and will therefore try to avoid.

Some rules, when broken, are more detrimental to the team than others. Kick a ball out of the way when peppering? Not good, but likely just a reflex. Give them a warning. Boot a ball across the gym after missing a dig? She's sitting out, no questions asked. Which leads me to my next point.

My personal approach to rule breaking is this: You break a rule, you sit out. Everyone knows the rules, and I don't have the time or patience to give warnings. In very rare circumstances, I'll give a warning. But because my teams know that I am a no-nonsense coach when it comes to breaking the rules, warnings are rarely necessary.

While different age groups will have different kinds of rule breaking, you need to decide on punishments which are consistent with your temperament and coaching style. I don't personally agree with punishments such as running lines/push-ups/laps/what have you. This gives those activities a negative connotation, and I want my girls to WANT to do those things to be in better shape.

I do make one exception to running as discipline, simply because a former coach of mine used it and I think it is genius.

Swearing was not allowed on the team, and if someone decided that they were going to cuss, the entire team would get mad at them. But why? Why would a player be mad at another player for breaking a rule?

Depending on the number of letters in the word of choice, that is how many laps the team had to run. But wait, it gets better.

The person who swore would stand in the middle of the court or gym and count the number of laps out loud for the rest of the team. My old coach used peer pressure against us to curb our attitudes. I can practically guarantee that if you implement this rule with your team, swearing will be minimal.

Whatever disciplinary policies you decide on, make sure you stay consistent in your enforcement of the rules. Just because one of the girls who has never once gotten in trouble is having a side conversation during a huddle, do not let it go. Fairness is something girls are very sensitive to, particularly when they feel it is going against them.

Giving off the perception of playing favorites can be just as damaging to their trust in you as if you were actually playing favorites.

PRACTICE DESIGN

One of the topics I am most passionate about when it comes to volleyball is practice design. Organizing skill practice and game-like drills in a way that builds up and culminates in proper skill execution is vital to running a successful practice. It is crucial that you spend more than just a few minutes coming up with practice until you are a seasoned coach (and even then, you'll probably spend more time tweaking drills to make practice just right).

So let's talk about practice design. What I mean by practice design is the flow of your practices from one major category of skill work/play/games/etc. on to the next. To begin, you always need to warm up. This should take roughly 10 minutes for each practice to make sure your girls have warmed up their muscles properly. The rest of how you spend your time will vary depending on how long your practices are (with younger players practicing for shorter amounts of time usually) and can be broken up as follows:

CHAPTER 4: BEGINNING OF THE SEASON

Dynamic stretching:

Stretches that make your players move.

Warm-up game:

A game that gets the players moving and playing volleyball, but eases them into play. This should not include scrimmaging and should limit full serves or attacking right way. Games with a lot of movement are ideal.

Skill demonstration/concept introduction:

Explain a new skill or concept. For this example, I'll use jousting. Jousting is when two players on opposing courts go up to direct a ball that is tight to the net and could end up on either side. This may be too advanced for younger teams, but is a good skill to practice above 12 and under or middle school volleyball. Explanations should take no longer than five minutes unless it is very complex.

Skill or concept specific drill:

Now you run a drill which focuses on the new skill or concept (in our case, jousting).

Ensure you are running a drill which is slowed down enough to focus on good technique, but quick enough to get a lot of touches on the ball and keep their attention.

Game-like activity which incorporates skill or concept:

Similar to the warm-up game, we're not getting into full-on scrimmage mode here. We just want to put the girls in a game situation which has everyone practicing jousting as if it were happening in the game. Playing a short court game where players can only tip will help the jousting situation arise more often.

Old/familiar skill demonstration:

Since jousting is not typically one of the first skills you cover, you are probably a few weeks or a month into your season by the time this comes up. Your team should be familiar with their defensive positions by now, so you can review defense at this time. Emphasize tip coverage, as this is related to jousting.

CHAPTER 4: BEGINNING OF THE SEASON

<u>Scrimmage which incorporates both skills and/or concepts</u>:

> Now is the time you get to test out how well your players have grasped the new information you have given them. By running a full scrimmage, you are allowing your players to get in the habit of implementing their new skills in a way that would naturally occur in a game, not one that is forced or predictable.

<u>Cool down</u>:

> Your players have probably put a lot of effort into the last 15-20 minutes of practice and need to ease into their normal state. Cool downs do not need to take very long, but should not be skipped.

*It is very important to incorporate water breaks for the team. If someone is thirsty during a drill, you should also allow them to get water right away. Schedule these in, but make sure your players know that they can get water at any time. This is a safety issue.

This does not, by any means, have to be followed religiously every practice. However, if you are struggling to create a schedule for your practice then this is a great place to start. Some nights you may also have skills which do not easily work together using this framework.

For example, you need to work on serving and setting. It can be hard to make these two skills mesh well using this practice design. Or you might need to spend an entire practice teaching serve receive. That's fine. Just keep in mind a few pointers when designing practices.

Remember to <u>keep explaining to a minimum</u>, unless it is a drill or concept which needs clarification and will be used multiple times throughout the season. Make sure skills practiced relate to any games played or are emphasized during scrimmages. Finally, <u>start with foundational skills and build your way up</u>. You can see where your players are at and might catch a few mistakes that would go unnoticed if you just jump into more advanced drills.

CHAPTER 5: YOUR FIRST MATCH OR TOURNAMENT

This is it. Your first test has arrived, and you couldn't be more excited! Although you've gone through a lot so far this season, you still have a few new obstacles to conquer. Creating lineups, worrying about playing time, and just making sure that everyone gets to the right facility can cause problems if not done correctly.

To have a successful first match or tournament, you should start planning for everything in this section about two weeks out. This gives you a week to get everything in line, and then the following week to disseminate the information and answer questions from players and parents.

A FEW PRACTICALITIES: FEES, PARKING, WEATHER, & MORE

The list of administrative tasks never really ends for volleyball coaches. While you're probably focused primarily on volleyball (line-ups, strategies, stats, etc.), your fans are going to need to know a few basics. You are the keeper of that information. The sooner you get this information out, the better! Here's what they're going to want to know:

Entrance fees:

> Often times big tournaments will be held in large venues. These are typically rented by the hosting team/association and will more than likely have an entrance fee imposed on spectators by the facility. This could range from $2-$10 per person, and often times only cash is accepted. Families will want to know this ahead of time so they're not running to the ATM that morning.

CHAPTER 5: YOUR FIRST MATCH OR TOURNAMENT

Parking:

> While it may seem unimportant to communicate parking information, this might make the difference between having all of your players there on time or not. Many times parents will be able to find their way when parking because they will just need to find all of the girls walking towards a certain location with their bags, pillows, and blankets.
>
> However, if you are playing in an urban location which has strict street parking laws, not knowing where to park will guarantee you have some cranky parents before your match starts! If the tournaments you are playing in do not provide you with parking information, make sure to follow-up before the tournament. This will give you peace of mind and your parents will thank you for it.

Weather:

> Volleyball is an indoor sport, so why worry about the weather, right? Wrong! Especially if you are traveling a few hours

away, parents are not likely to know if there will be weather that is less than desirable. Snow, rain, and fog could all slow down the drive (or even make it unsafe, in which case you should seriously consider canceling). Rain and puddles walking into the facility could make a few parents angry, and bad weather on the return trip might encourage parents to get a hotel rather than drive through storms. It won't impact your play, but it's all about keeping your parents happy.

Food:

Practically all facilities which sell food do not allow you to bring in your own food. This is important to communicate with your parents because then they will know that if they still end up making food for their daughters, they will have to go out to the car to eat.

If a location sells food, it will likely be cash only, so highly recommend that the families bring cash. Starving players are no fun to be around, and parents who spent the morning prepping food, only to find out they can't bring it into the tournament, will be angry. Clarify this with the tournament director if it is not included in their information packet which they send to you.

You'll need food too, so don't forget about yourself. You will often be the busiest person from your team, so make sure you schedule a time to eat. A growling stomach is very distracting during the third set of a match late in the day.

Other:

While parking, entrance fees, food restrictions, and weather are major topics which you need to communicate with your parents for every tournament, some facilities will have additional restrictions which will also need to be communicated to your parents.

Occasionally there are facilities which will not allow you to bring in chairs. This is to lessen congestion in walkways, avoid fire hazards, and even to protect new flooring. Regardless, it is no fun to pack in a camp chair only to find out you need to take it back to the car.

Many locations will also restrict the players to only having water on the bench. This is to avoid sticky messes when sport drinks get spilled, but is annoying to the players and parents when all they bring is their favorite electrolyte-filled water alternative. You can get around this by filling solid water bottles with something other than water, but if it spills you'll be caught and may get some sort of penalty.

All facilities are different, and there could very well be other restrictions which are not on this list. Make sure to read the information packet which is sent to you by tournament directors before each tournament. I even encourage just forwarding this information to your parents (you'll have their emails if you followed my "Preseason Preparation" instructions).

WARM-UPS

So you get to your first tournament and you claim your spot to put all of your pillows and bags down and everyone starts to get ready.

CHAPTER 5: YOUR FIRST MATCH OR TOURNAMENT

Parents disappear to hunt down coffee and bathrooms, your libero is missing a kneepad, and you've already tripped over a backpack or two. You have to escape this mess! You walk over to the court where you know you are playing first and instruct the only player who followed you to run and get everyone else. They finally all come over, with their eyes only half open and yawning every 10 seconds. You instruct them to pepper and get loose while you wait for the ref to call for captains.

Now the exciting part: You lose the toss, but get "receive" (first kill!) and are off the court for the first nine minutes while the other team warms up. And then panic strikes. What are you going to do for nine whole minutes off the court!? Better yet, what are you going to do when you get ON the court!? This is a serious problem.

You quickly think back to high school. What did your team do in warm-ups? You then make your best attempt at running a drill that you did five, ten, maybe even fifteen years prior, and you can't quite figure it out. This is a small-scale disaster. Not only are you now out of focus for your match, your girls are also confused and not feeling confident in their abilities, and even worse, your competence. If this is the situation you find yourself in, you are practically guaranteed at least one loss for the day. And it's going to be that first match. You know how when you start your day in a bad mood, it's hard to get into a better mood? The same holds true for volleyball. Don't start your girls out on the wrong foot.

The rest of your day will be spent doing damage control. Planning out warm-ups at least two weeks before your first tournament is the best way to avoid this disaster. A few practices before your first tournament, decide what your warm-ups will be and how you will do them, then run through them with your team. I have some warm-up examples on my website at www.getthepancake.com that get touches on the ball for everyone and mimic game-like conditions if you need some suggestions.

Let them know that the drill you decide on will be warm-ups at tournaments for the rest of the year. These warm-ups should be game-like while also getting everyone loosened up and easing into volleyball.

They will probably fail the first time through

CHAPTER 5: YOUR FIRST MATCH OR TOURNAMENT

and make minimal progress. However, the second time that you run through this drill at your following practice you will see great improvement. Finally, at the last practice before your tournament, you should conduct warm-ups in this manner to improve their confidence in the warm-up. Follow this advice and your first tournament concerns will get off to a good start.

LINEUPS

A lot of coaches will enter into games with a predetermined line-up. Every game starts with the same lineup, and it is only ever changed if someone is sick, late, or hurt. On the other end of the spectrum, some coaches will come up with lineups on the spot, often thinking of them as they are turning in their lineup to the scorer's table before the match starts.

Each method has their advantages and disadvantages, so you need to think about which method will work best for you. This is one of the areas of coaching which doesn't impact your team TOO dramatically, but can still have some minor side effects if not carried out properly.

Having a set lineup for every match is better suited for older and more advanced teams. At higher levels you are likely playing to win, so a predetermined lineup makes sense. You will have decided through practice who works best next to one another, who understands their position the best, and who functions as a great substitute.

Your team will know what to expect and can focus on strictly playing volleyball rather than wondering if they're going to start or not, or how to play next to a different person than they're used to. While this works well for more advanced teams, a younger team could also benefit from a consistent lineup when they are learning their positions.

Mixing up the rotation has a few advantages as well, such as teaching your players to work with everyone on the team instead of only being able to play next to a certain player.

I believe this is most beneficial for younger club teams since the goal (at least for my teams) hasn't ever been strictly winning, it has been to learn. Learning a new position or learning to play next to someone new is more beneficial in the younger years.

Then, when your middle blocker suddenly gets to high school and becomes an outside hitter, she will have an idea of what she's doing. She will have more value for her future teams because you taught her to play multiple positions.

A downside to mixing up the lineup is that there can be a lot of confusion. Like, a lot. In a match, it's very possible to have the other team score three points in a row before your left back figures out she's the one who is supposed to be covering those shots to the middle of the court which are destroying your defense.

Or you may have a middle who is learning outside, but falls back into her old habits and suddenly you've got two confused middle blockers and no outside.

Know yourself and your coaching style. Are you ok with last minute lineup creations? Do you need to have everything planned out the night before? Will you come up with your own creative version of the two extremes?

If last-minute planning stresses you out, save

yourself the headache and come up with your lineups the night before. If you know you're going to just change your mind anyway, don't put yourself through that and just do your thing.

PLAYING TIME

This is one of the touchiest subjects in all of coaching. How are you going to manage playing time for all of your players? Are you going to play everyone equally, regardless of how they practice and perform? Will you only play the best players, and make substitutions only when, say, a good front row player rotates into the back row? Will you attempt some combination of the two?

This should already be decided before you start coaching, and will depend on the club you coach for, the level of play, etc. If you are coaching an elite 18U club team where the goal is to get players into college programs, you're probably only going to play the players who are best at certain positions (although at this level, there shouldn't be too much of a difference between your best and worst players).

On the flip side, when you're coaching 7th

CHAPTER 5: YOUR FIRST MATCH OR TOURNAMENT

graders on the middle school B team, you might (and should!) have different priorities when it comes to playing time. These girls, after all, are playing at one of the lowest (though not least important!) levels of volleyball, and the desire to win by you, the coach, should not be higher than the desire to teach volleyball skills to the girls you coach.

A word of caution: I have played against teams at the 14U level where girls were not subbed out for an entire tournament, and other girls just seemed to "ride the pine." While I understand that this happens during championship matches and during other highly competitive events, this should not be commonplace at the 14U or 12U level, whether you are ranked #6 or #126.

I get it. Not every player has the skills to play at a high level, but YOU picked them to be on your team, and you owe them a little respect. Never guarantee playing time, and make the players work for it, but it shouldn't be withheld. This will wreck your team chemistry and create divisions between the girls which you won't be aware of, but you will definitely play a role in causing them.

Can you tell that my vote is for a balance between playing everyone equally and only playing the best players? My stance on this comes from the saying, "you're only as good as your weakest link." If you do nothing to get your "weakest link" out there in games and building confidence, you're doing a disservice to the rest of your team.

By building the skills and confidence of your subs, you're raising the level of competition you have at practice, which allows your team to succeed against higher ranked teams using more of your roster. It's a win-win, really. Yet most coaches crave the win and sacrifice long-term development for an immediate victory.

The important concept to remember here is to be aware of your stance on playing time before the season begins, and hold that philosophy throughout the year. Changing your philosophy halfway through the year is a huge no-no. Unless you've really been screwing things up and figure out how to fix them, I don't suggest making changes. Players and parents get accustomed to one way of coaching, and by changing things up, you are only setting yourself up for controversy.

CHAPTER 5: YOUR FIRST MATCH OR TOURNAMENT

REFEREEING

Refereeing is one of those tasks that you have to do as a coach, but don't necessarily want to. You will typically get your basic training done through your volleyball association after you join a club where you go and learn how to keep score, track the libero, and some other general refereeing technicalities for both the up-ref and down- ref.

When it comes to tournament time, if you are a head coach you will most likely assume the role of up ref and if you are an assistant coach you will most likely be the down ref, although these are not requirements. It often comes down to preference, unless you are at a higher level tournament where refs are provided for you. Although this organization of referees is common, sometimes as a head coach I will have my assistant coach be the up ref and I will be the down ref, which helps as a training tool for the assistant if they want to be a head coach someday. Other times, I will switch out my assistant coach for a player who is working on furthering her skills. This gives the assistant a break and also gives the players great leadership experience.

At the final practice before a tournament, it is a good idea to assign refereeing jobs so that they are fair and expectations are set. My first year, I made the mistake of asking who wanted to do lines, score keep, etc. right before our first match that we had to ref. This was a disaster and all of the girls who had to do lines were pouting, some people got away with doing significantly less work than others, and some didn't get a break because they volunteered every time. By assigning refereeing jobs ahead of time, everyone knows what their responsibilities will be and they believe the system is fair, which minimizes complaining (always nice when you're spending 12 hours a day with them).

Now that you're all prepared to ref, you've actually got to get your hands dirty and do the thing. It's very important to be calm your first time when you are reffing. I remember the first time that I was reffing, and on the very first serve actually, I missed four hits on a side. Luckily it went into the net so I was able to play it off, but my nerves definitely got the best of me.

You also have to be confident, and one of the

CHAPTER 5: YOUR FIRST MATCH OR TOURNAMENT

ways to do that is by knowing the rules. Make sure that you read the rulebook your association gives you and study it. Not only will this help you be a better coach, but when you are reffing it will also help you make more confident calls. Fake it till you make it definitely holds true here, because some coaches are just complete jerks and will argue with you and try to make you feel stupid. Never give in, even if you're not sure, or else you're setting yourself up to be walked all over.

If the other coach really wants to prove you are wrong, they can challenge your call. This is a lengthy process and it is rarely ever worth it to a coach, especially in the early tournaments when you're likely to have less confidence. If this does happen and you get overruled... So what. You learn, you move on, and you beat that team when it's your turn to play them.

Another hint for effective reffing is to make sure that you are watching both teams when they warm up. This will help you understand their skill level and make judgments as to how tightly you're going to have to make calls. Make sure that you keep your calls consistent with the expectations of different playing levels. If you are refereeing 14 and under club volleyball, you're going to be making different calls than you would for high school varsity volleyball.

Make sure that you are making stricter calls in the beginning of a match, rather than allowing the game to get sloppier and sloppier until you can't stand it and have to call a double on the setter who has been setting poorly the entire game. This will likely be at the end of a close match, and you will definitely get a lively response from the coaches, bench, and parents. Having people boo at you does not feel good.

You can avoid the booing by making strict calls early on, where they will merely elicit a grumble from a few of the more irritable parents. The players will adjust their playing style, and there will be minimal issues moving forward. This is a hard lesson to learn on your own, and I advise you to follow my suggestions. But if you must, experience will surely make a quick learner out of you in this area.

A final note on reffing: Keep it fun! I know, I know… How can this be done? No one EVER talks about reffing as being a fun task. How many times have you, as a player, seen refs who were having fun? Well, just because other people don't do it, doesn't mean you can't!

For example, when you go through training, you will be taught that there are certain signals which scorekeepers are supposed to give the up ref when they are done recording a substitution or other events. This is a simple two arms up motion, which I rarely see teams do, opting instead for a head nod or eye contact. I have my girls do the motion every time, not only because I know it means they are truly done writing, but we also recognize that it is a little silly and share a small laugh every time. This keeps my score table happy and engaged in the game.

I love my line judges even more. Have you ever seen the line judges for college volleyball, where they stand completely still until they need to make a call, and when they make the call, they whip their flag to indicate in or out, and strike somewhat exaggerated poses? I make my girls do this as well. For starters, it makes me laugh. They also think it's funny. Although not everyone buys into it, most of my teams do. And again, it keeps them engaged.

Finally, when you see a 13-year-old whip their flag to make a call, you're not going to argue with her. Parents and crowds, in general, can be downright atrocious towards the reffing team if they disagree with a call. And they WILL disagree if a 4'9" twig is weakly calling the ball in while shrugging her shoulders and looking at the up-ref as if asking if she's right. Make them be ridiculous. They'll be more confident in their calls, you'll stay entertained, and reffing won't be as much of a chore as it would be otherwise.

CHAPTER 6: MAKING DECISIONS THROUGH DATA

Keeping statistics on your team's performance during matches and tournaments is very important. Have you heard the saying, "You manage what you measure?" This holds true in all sports and volleyball is no different.

While keeping stats can be very consuming during a match, finding a way to keep them is important for in-game decisions, practice design, and growth over a season. Not only can you learn the progress of individual players, but you can also track trends for your team. This chapter will discuss what you need to consider when tracking stats and how to use the data you generate.

THE ART OF KEEPING STATS

Volleyball is such a fast-paced sport; it can be difficult to determine which stats you will actually be able to keep track of during a game while still coaching your players. Passing is important, but to what level do you track passing? Whether it was a good pass or not? What if it was a dig? Do you and your other coach agree on what a dig even is?

Head coaches and assistant coaches alike should understand how the team's stats will be kept, and depending on their age and your team culture, you may even want your players to understand your stats tracking system. I have found during games, the following stats can be kept while remaining sane and engaged in the game, with the ability to quickly note rally results and coach between serves.

Serves:

- In
- Out
- Ace
- Jump serve

Passing:

- Shank or dropped ball
- Passed up and playable
- Towards the setter
- To the setter

Sets:

- Set an attacker can hit
- Set an attacker cannot hit
- Assist

Attacks:

- Hit in
- Hit out/in the net
- Kill
- Tip
- Kill from tip
- Downball
- Kill from downball

This is a lot of information! But believe me, you can track it all with a little practice. I have found that freshman in high school are able to keep these stats, though I would not ask players any younger to keep them.

Some coaches may be wary to hand the task of keeping stats over to their players. I don't recommend doing this right away, as the beginning of the year is a time for them to get familiar with a coach's coaching style. Once your players understand what a "tip kill" really means, they will be able to keep track on their own.

Does bias enter the picture? Not if you have everything defined clearly. Passing is about the only area which can be a judgment call, but you immediately have to watch for the next touch on a ball, so your hurry to keep up with the action will cancel out most bias. You can also have your stats keeper sit next to you and call out the score as it happens.

While I encourage you to make your own stat sheet, I have a free example available in the "Coaches Resources" section of my website at www.getthepancake.com. This template has

CHAPTER 6: MAKING DECISIONS THROUGH DATA

space for tracking all of the above-mentioned stats, a key for the above-mentioned stats, and room to create your own.

YOU HAVE DATA... NOW WHAT?

Let's say you are a club coach, and you have just finished up your first tournament. You are exhausted, your body aches, and you're starving. After getting home at 9:00pm from your tournament, you immediately crash. When you wake up sore but well rested, you are excited to check out your stats from the day before!

You stare at the two sheets of paper which contain every touch on the ball from the day before (the ones you could keep up with anyway) and start combing through the data. You meticulously crunch the numbers and start to see a picture form.

Without the stats, you feel that your team did well. They finished 5th overall. Their pool play performance was not the best, but it was your first tournament and you were able to win all of your matches after lunch during bracket play.

During lunch, you peeked at your stats and saw that some of your best players were missing their serves. So you made a few tweaks to your substitutions and this worked out for you. Without the stats, things would have stayed the same, and you may or may not have seen the afternoon success which transpired.

As you enter your stats into the Excel sheet, you discover even more insights into the team's performance from the day before. Overall, your team had 70% of their attacks go in. You also notice that there are a lot of "bad sets" marked for your second setter in most of your lineups.

You also notice that, despite your promise and belief that equal playing time is important, one of your players had significantly fewer touches on the ball than everyone else. You realize that you were reluctant to get this player in after the morning was off to such a poor start, and didn't notice during your lunch break.

Finally, you see that your team had mostly passes which the setter could get to, but were not directly to the setter. While you know they are learning, you also think the percentage of perfect passes should be higher.

CHAPTER 6: MAKING DECISIONS THROUGH DATA

IMPROVEMENT THROUGH DATA

Armed with your percentages, the wheels begin to turn. Clearly, the team needs to improve their passing. Was it a lack of movement to the ball? Poor form? Lack of understanding positions? Miscommunication?

And your setter. Does she need to push the ball higher? Out further? Switch up her sets? Change her footwork?

Are your hitters swinging at balls they should be chipping or tipping instead? While aggressiveness is one thing, poor decision making is another.

While the numbers will tell you information you are often not aware of, you are usually able to fill in the blanks through your intuition. You know the passing will get better through the season because the girls just don't understand your defensive system yet.

You noticed your setter's footwork was off right from the beginning but were not able to get her to correct it during the tournament. And your swingers were too excited to go for the big kill during their first tournament.

However, instead of just continuing to practice without consulting these stats may have led you to focus on improving your serving, which, after a full analysis of the data, was not the underlying issue for most of your points which were lost.

Through data, you will be able to identify areas of weakness, as well as strength, and improve your team through training specifically designed to correct for deficiencies.

DATA-DRIVEN DRILL DESIGN

While it is easy to look at a low overall hitting percentage and decide you need to work on your attacking, running through hitting lines at your next practice may boost performance, but there is so much more you can do through the use of your data to design better drills.

Using the running example in this chapter, let's think about drills which could work on solving most of these issues by breaking them down using the numbers we gathered, and our understanding of the problem by using this table:

CHAPTER 6: MAKING DECISIONS THROUGH DATA

PROBLEM	REASON
Passing at 55%	Confused during defense
Setting at 75%	Footwork off
Attacking at 70%	Going for kills

Instead of focusing on the problem, we shift our attention to corrective action by determining the cause of the problem. This puts us in a place where we can solve issues instead of ruminate on them.

You do not want to combine an entire week's worth of learning into one drill (unless you only practice once a week), so focus on only one or two aspects of the game which will improve your problem areas. Drills which are centered around these concepts will lead to a natural progression which is integrated sooner than an onslaught of new skills which will be forgotten next week.

So how could we take these skills and create a drill which will improve these areas? A quick search online may return some good results. I like to reinvent the wheel though, and try to create my own drills so I know exactly which skills will be targeted.

Let's test this out. Try to think of a drill in which your entire team could participate where the focus is on defensive positioning. Remember, try to make it as game-like as possible. Take a few minutes and sketch it out.

NOTE: How you sketch out your drill is not important. As long as you are able to read it and remember what it means both at tomorrow's practice and at the end of the season, you're doing it right. Making notes can be helpful, as can writing down WHY you're doing a certain drill.

Ok, so you have your defensive drill designed. Does it reinforce behaviors which you noticed were lacking at the tournament? Is it easy to explain? What new jargon is being introduced to reinforce these behaviors?

Answer these questions and reevaluate your drill. Make changes if necessary.

Now, can you add another element to the drill

to solve another problem? Try to work either the setter's footwork or attacking problem into the drill.

CONSTANT TRACKING

Keeping stats once or twice is not enough to sufficiently monitor your progress over a season. There have been matches where, if I ran out of stat sheets, I drew one out on the back of a score sheet from the scorer's table. The stats sheets provide so much information, not only on the day's performance, but on progress over a season.

While I am in the habit of keeping stats at every tournament and always have it at the top of my pile of papers on my clipboard, some of you may forget while you're getting into the habit. If you're coaching for a school team and forget to keep stats for one game, it's probably not the end of the world. If your players have grown accustomed to your stats reporting, however, they may be disappointed. Particularly if they played a great match. But one game won't derail your stats-keeping effort.

During club, forgetting stats for a whole

tournament might have a bigger impact on your ability to coach using data. If you remember a few matches in that you haven't been keeping stats, I would suggest you pick up where you're at instead of saying "oh well," and carrying on. In club, your opportunities to track progress are much more limited, so you should use every opportunity you have.

Keeping track of statistics throughout the season will not only allow you to see team and individual progress, you will also be able to make objective decisions regarding playing time and lineups.

Although I tend to discourage discussing these topics with parents, it's much easier to back up your decisions when you can show that a player has not been performing at a level compared to someone who maybe took their place in the lineup. Use stats sparingly in this manner, but it is nice to know you have them as a backup.

CHAPTER 7: MID-SEASON REFLECTION

You've got half of your matches or tournaments under your belt at this point. You can sort of figure out where your team is headed as far as rankings in their league or division, and you've got a good grip on your players' strengths and weaknesses. And while things have been going great up to this point, you're starting to see a few things emerge from the shadows.

Some players aren't progressing how you thought they would, and they're getting less playing time than you'd like. But they've also accepted that position, and aren't trying as hard in practice. Or the opposite, they aren't trying as hard at practice, yet they are expecting more playing time regardless.

A few parents are starting to get upset with your

leadership over the season. Although you're well prepared and know what needs to get done, maybe you forgot to bring the ball bag to one of the tournaments. Or practices the last few nights have gone over by about ten minutes each time, and they claim that you do not respect their schedule.

And when you announce to your players that you're going to play Swordfish tonight (a real drill named by one of my former players), only two or three are excited and the rest do not hide their dissatisfaction, while slumping their shoulders and exclaiming, "Again!? We play that all the time!"

These are real struggles you will face, some hopefully less than others. By knowing that these are totally normal, hopefully they will not deflate your enthusiasm for coaching, but rather indicate to you that it is time to mix things up.

KEEP AN EYE OUT FOR BURNOUT

The dirty B word. It can happen to anyone, at any time, and for any number of reasons. Burnout is characterized by less energy, less excitement, and often times, a desire to quit.

This is a very real concern and can affect anyone on your team. Burnout is just as likely to impact players who are juggling many activities and multiple sports, as it is to impact the girls who have been playing volleyball year round for the last 5 years.

One of the hardest things about burnout is that often the solution is to take a break. In the middle of your season, this is the last thing you want to have happen. By noticing when enthusiasm or excitement is starting to drop in individuals, often having a conversation with them can be enough to lift them out of it.

Pay attention to your team. If you are not naturally attentive to this type of thing, try to find an assistant or head coach who fills in this gap for you. If you're the only coach, approach a parent who attends every practice and get their opinion on how things are going. This could open a can of worms, so be sure to phrase your question as very specific and a one-time question.

If you notice some players are showing up later and later, or are dragging their feet when they used to be one of the most enthusiastic players, you may have a case of burnout on your hands. Completely missing practices can be a huge warning sign as well, particularly if no reasons are given or they are unexcused absences.

Remember, you can only do so much when a player reaches this stage. If you do not switch up their routine or make changes to get them out of this mindset, you likely won't see them on the court next year. Discuss with parents whenever you think burnout could be a problem. Do your research on burnout prior to this discussion, so that you can offer up-to-date solutions and offer to help where possible.

TEAM AND INDIVIDUAL PROGRESS

Using your stats, you should be able to track your team's progress up to this point, both as a group and individually. This is why keeping stats is highly encouraged, regardless of age or skill level. You can see how everyone is doing, and hopefully, they are getting better.

Wins and losses can only tell you so much about how your team is doing, and can rarely give you deep insight into the development of a specific player.

CHAPTER 7: MID-SEASON REFLECTION

To begin assessing the team's progress from the beginning of the season up until the midpoint, look at major stats, such as passing, setting, attacking, and service percentages. Do you see a gradual increase from the beginning of the year? Younger teams should see sharper increases in skills, whereas a more advanced and older team might make significant improvements in play, yet only see an increase in skills by a few percentage points.

The important thing to see in the trends is progression. Maybe at one or two matches or tournaments you have a drop in percentage, but depending on the skill level of the other teams this may be expected on some levels.

For individuals, you will also want to see a progression in skills. Consider any changes in position or maybe even family events which may have negatively impacted performance. Changes in position could also positively impact stats if a change was made to better utilize their particular skill set.

Regardless of whether or not you are analyzing team or individual stats, the goal should not strictly be to see a bump in numbers. Sure, we

WANT to see that, because that shows we are getting better in certain areas. But we want to be able to paint a clear picture of where we are at.

Seeing stats drop between your first tournament and your second could show either a change in competition levels, the absence of a star player, attempts to play at a higher level, or even playing to a lower level. Notes are so important for stats so that you can have a clear idea in your mind of what direction the team is moving in. Progress doesn't need to equal better numbers, but it should be clear in your story that your team is moving forward and improving.

CHECK-IN WITH HIGHER UPS

It has probably been awhile since you've last seen your boss, unless you are an assistant coach reporting to a head coach, or if your boss's daughter is on the team. If some time has passed since you last checked-in with your athletic director or club director, schedule a time to sit down with them and review how things are going.

This does not need to be a formal meeting where you go into their office with reports in hand, but could simply be meeting up for coffee or lunch, or even just a 10 to 15-minute phone call to discuss how things are going.

Setting up a meeting shows you are dedicated to carrying out the club or school's mission because you are checking in to make sure you are on track and aligned with the goals of your organization. While you should know that you are on track **BEFORE** scheduling this meeting, make some last minute tweaks if you realize that you are veering away from the mission.

Be prepared to discuss how the overall team is progressing, and share a few highlights of individuals. If you feel comfortable, you can share a struggle that you have, but you should have an idea of how you're going to correct it before you bring it up in front of your boss.

If you have an issue which you know parents are talking about, you should definitely bring this up and clear the air, because if you know that parents are talking about something, you can pretty much guarantee your higher-ups have heard about it as well. By explaining from a coach's point of view, your boss will be able to have your back if any parents or family members approach them about this topic.

Remember: You are not complaining here or sharing everything you know. This person is not your BFF, but your boss. Keep the conversation professional, and make a good impression. This will show that you have the ability to be a great leader, and will instantly build credibility with them which will be useful in future seasons.

REFRESH DRILLS

I am a fan of running consistently scheduled and predictable practices. This means I'll use the same warm-up drill every practice, usually end with a scrimmage, and only the skills we work on between the two is what changes. I think this is a great setup, which is discussed in the Practice Design section.

But once in a while, you've got to mix things up. Especially in the middle of the year and towards the end, the girls will get tired of the same practice agenda. It's predictable, and it can get boring. At this point in the season, mixing it up can be a good thing.

CHAPTER 7: MID-SEASON REFLECTION

Research some new warm-up ideas online or in other books on coaching volleyball (but seriously, online is free, start there). This is a great place to start, and new warm-up drills especially will set the tone for fun.

Keep in mind, you are wanting to incorporate the fun aspects of volleyball. While you will have one or two girls who absolutely love passing (thank goodness for them and whatever planet they came from), it would be ideal to incorporate some form of attacking or serving into your "for fun" drills. Everyone likes to hit, and everyone likes to serve. If you can do one or both, you're golden. Give the drill a fun name and it'll be even better.

While you are trying to reignite the love of the game at this point in the season by adding a little bit of silliness, keep the focus on volleyball.

Stick to working on proper form and actual volleyball skills, and maybe only give up a little on game-like situations if you have to. You still want to be practicing skills you will use in upcoming matches and tournaments, so I do not recommend completely abandoning volleyball in favor of basketball or dodgeball to liven things up. (Side note: I'm horrible at basketball and dislocated my pinky playing dodgeball, so take that advice with a grain of salt).

You could also ask the girls which games they would like to play, but just realize that this could backfire. They may start arguing about which game to play, and it could be split down the middle. You will then have to choose, and half of the girls will complain while the other half tries to prove how much fun they're having. Comical in hindsight, but annoying at the time.

Overall, I recommend just researching your own drills and bringing in a few fun ones to try. Or, if you're a head coach, give an assistant the opportunity to run practice. This will likely change the entire vibe of practice and may be just what your players need. Assistant coaches tend to be more fun (I'm a head coach and will admit this) so usually just giving them the reins for a practice once or twice a month will be enough to revive tired players. You will also contribute to your assistant's development, and that will give you warm fuzzies.

CHAPTER 8: MAJOR END OF THE YEAR EVENTS

You made it! The end of the year is here, and you are filled with excitement, a few jitters, and a healthy dose of anxiety. A lot rides on the end of the year. Whether you are hosting your last home match, competing in play-in rounds for the state tournament, or heading off to regionals, there are extra steps you should take to ensure success during this important time of year.

From the pressures you will face from administrators and parents to perform at a high level to the internal pressures you'll face telling you to change everything completely, keep in mind that you've already made all of the possible preparations.

Your middle won't suddenly grow three inches taller (unless you're coaching 8th graders... then even four inches is possible), your libero won't suddenly become more aggressive, and your setter isn't going to become any louder and in-control of the court.

This isn't meant to be disheartening. It is meant to keep you in a frame of mind which is grounded in reality. You have done the best you could up until this point, and how the final matches unfold will reveal to you the values and behaviors which you have instilled in your players.

There is only one technical winner at the end of the day. Maybe it's you, maybe it isn't. The important thing to remember here is your definition of success.

Remember way back to the section on coaching philosophy? When you defined what success meant to you and even wrote down what you'd be working towards this season? That is what you're striving for.

Maybe your definition of success was to share the love of the game with your team. While this is much harder to technically measure than, say,

CHAPTER 8: MAJOR END OF THE YEAR EVENTS

improve your stats every tournament, you can tell if you have achieved it by feeling the pulse of your team leading into the final event.

Are they all excited? Are some just ready for the season to be over? Are they ALL ready for the season to be over? I hope you achieve your definition of success, whatever it is, and are able to go into your final match confident that you had a great season.

By making sure you take care of these few final tasks and checking in with yourself and other coaches, you'll be set up for achieving your success.

PREP WORK

As I already mentioned, you've done all you can up to this point, practice-wise. That doesn't mean, however, that the last week or two of practice should be just about having fun. While you'll be hard-pressed to find a team who will complain about playing fun games, what the girls want isn't always best for them.

The last couple of weeks of practice, you should focus on skill refinement and keeping things fresh (read the Refresh Drills section for more information). At this point, you want to be introducing relatively few new concepts, so the team can focus on getting better at what they know and being confident in their skills, rather than head into their final match punching each other while trying to swing block or tripping over their feet because you've been working on new plays.

My viewpoint on "fun" has always been that strong execution is what makes playing fun. So spice up practice by playing a game you don't play often, but that your team absolutely loves. Get them running hard and sweating, and even though they may be exhausted at the time, they will love it.

When we discuss keeping your coaching style consistent a few sections forward from now, apply that information to your practices as well. To summarize: If you've always ran hard practices, continue to do so. If you've always had fun, game-centered practices, continue to do so. As I said, this will be discussed later. But is important to think about now.

OVER-COMMUNICATE WITH FAMILIES

The end of the season is an exciting time for parents, yet is usually stressful as well. Regionals can mean driving 5 hours away and staying two or three nights in a hotel. State playoffs can mean last-minute babysitters for siblings and missing a little sister's softball tournament.

By communicating updates as they come in, unless there is a high likelihood that something will change, you are helping your team go into the end of the season with much more calm families and a real focus on volleyball.

If you follow the advice given in the Beginning of the Year section on what to communicate with families, you'll be in good shape. For some teams, the end of the year can be a confusing time. Maybe you will be entering state playoffs? Or going to Regionals or Nationals? Often times, the information you need to share with families is incomplete or will not be determined until after play begins. Let families know all of the information that you have, and create a few scenarios for them so they can plan ahead as well.

Email, discuss at practice, and be available for phone calls. Make sure you know all different angles which parents might come at you from, because they will ask twice as many questions leading up to your last match.

MAKE IT SPECIAL

The day has finally arrived. And although you've done your best to keep things normal and consistent leading into your final day of competition, you do need to recognize that it is a special event which demands a small celebration.

Regardless of your coaching philosophy, whether you consider yourself more of a drill sergeant than a cheerleader, take the time to do something special for the girls. This could be as simple as bringing snacks for the day, or as time-consuming as doing a craft project of your choice.

Later on, you'll have time to really celebrate every player at an awards banquet. However, it's still nice to set aside a time during a break in your last tournament to give a little thank you speech to your team and their families. Share a

CHAPTER 8: MAJOR END OF THE YEAR EVENTS

few of your favorite memories and try to include as many players as possible.

I recommend doing this during a break in the middle of the day so that you do not wait until the end of the day when there is potential that you do not end your tournament on a high note. Giving a thank you speech after a loss won't be as well received as when everyone still sees potential in how the day will go.

If you are coaching a high school or middle school program, you can do a small speech before the beginning of your last match. You may have a lot to say and want to get super emotional and deep, but save this for later when they don't have to turn around and get into game-mode right away.

You should prepare your speech, even if it is only 30 seconds long. Let's just acknowledge now that we are all long-winded and tend to over-explain things and drag speeches out. What you need at this point in time is a succinct but heartfelt message to inspire your players. Keep it short, meaningful, and applicable to all players. That is the way to give a good speech before a final match.

A WARNING: KEEP YOUR COACHING STYLE CONSISTENT

Regionals. State Playoffs. Conference Championships. These are high-intensity events, and they will challenge even more experienced coaches. Whether your coaching style has been to play to win at all costs, or to get everyone the most playing time, suddenly doing a 180 at the final event for the season is a huge no-no, yet so many coaches do it.

But why?

Let's say you are a coach who has been playing to win all year. You're coaching a high school varsity team and have had success, and are ranked 3rd in your conference for wins. While winning is important to you, you realize that it is the last home game, and you have a senior on your team who has never started, let alone played very often.

So, during your last home match, you decided to make it up to her. She will start! She plays middle, and so that is where you want her to be. In order to get her into the lineup, you have to take out another senior. She has started all year,

CHAPTER 8: MAJOR END OF THE YEAR EVENTS

so you don't think this will be a huge issue. You are imagining the joy of the senior who always sat out, and anticipating excitement from your team.

When your team has finished warm-ups, and everyone is in the huddle ready for their usual assignments, you announce the lineup change! And while the player who is now starting is very excited at first, the rest of the team looks at you with questioning eyes. Your normal starter is visibly shaken, and the new starter is now uncomfortable from the tension in the air.

The whistle blows, your team says a cheer, and they take the court. The first serve is passed up, but the new player gets in the setter's way, likely due to nerves and game inexperience. The next serve goes to your new starter, which results in a double hit and the loss of an opportunity to sideout. The third serve is then shanked by one of your normal starters because she is trying to help the new starter get into position and there is mistrust between the two. You see the frustration building, and so you sub in your normal starter. The team is able to make a play and eventually win the serve, but there is a noticeable difference in your team's attitude.

While there was only one small change in the lineup from the entire year, it was not an earned lineup change which warranted confidence from the other players, and it was against the coaching style the team had come to rely on. Remember when we discussed trust way back in the Preseason Preparation section? Any trust you had you just destroyed. And win or lose this game, it will affect your play-in rounds for the state tournament.

The same can be said for coaches who play for fun all year, and then think they owe it to the girls to go out and win! So they play only the best players during the final game or tournament, abandoning the culture and trust which they worked so hard to build throughout the entire season.

While it may be hard to stick to your coaching philosophy when the season is coming to an end, you need to stick with what is expected. Unless you have some event which warrants a drastic change (a player is unable to attend a major match, a normal sub has outworked a starter and is it is best for the team to have them in, your club director or athletic director asks you to change your style), just stick with what you've been doing.

If you think you may have issues sticking with a certain style at the end of the year, reevaluate your coaching philosophy with that in mind.

CHAPTER 9: CELEBRATIONS AND AWARDS

You've made it! Your first season of coaching is now under your belt. This is a bittersweet time because the experience is over, but hopefully it was a ton of fun and you created a lot of great memories.

Before your responsibilities as "coach" are officially over, there is still one task to perform. An end of the year celebration which highlights significant contributions made by your players throughout the year, and where achievements can be remembered.

Planning this may come more naturally to you if you like to host gatherings often, but this section is still worth a read because it addresses volleyball-specific issues you may run into.

LOGISTICS

OK, party planning basics. You will need the following:

- A date and time
- A venue
- Food and drinks
- Plates/paper towels/utensils/cups
- Parking options
- Entertainment
- Guests

Pretty simple, right?

It is, until you forget something in your rush to clean the house/pick up the trophies/order the pizza.

At least a week before your final tournament or match, you should determine all of the above logistics. This way, during the final week of practices you will be able to tell your team what the plans are for any celebrations and they can make arrangements to be there. Give at least two weeks' notice if it will be immediately following a final tournament. I recommend

CHAPTER 9: CELEBRATIONS AND AWARDS

giving them a week, however.

When you are deciding on the venue, take into account whether you want the ceremony to be large and formal, with parents and families in attendance as well, or if you just want your players to come and celebrate together.

As a player, my awards ceremonies were usually in a large group setting. The entire club would host an awards ceremony one night at the main school where practices were held and set up lunch tables in the cafeteria for players and families. Our own teams would sometimes have additional awards ceremonies afterward, but typically we just went to the one event.

As a coach, I have hosted smaller celebrations in my home with my assistant coaches helping me. These gatherings did not typically include parents, however, they have never been explicitly asked not to attend. If you'd like to make the event more family-friendly, I suggest specifically stating that in your invitations to the team. And please make sure you have enough seating and can fit everyone!

If you are hosting a large event, consider getting a catering company or bringing in lots of pizza (or sandwiches, etc.) which are easily picked up by guests and fairly inexpensive for the club or school. My high school made their fall sports awards ceremony a potluck, which worked well but there could be more headaches with this if it is your first time organizing.

Smaller events for just your team at your home are easily made into a potluck if you have families accompanying the players, but you can also just order a few pizzas for them and they should be fine. Girls can scarf down a lot of pizza, so better to order an extra cheese pizza and ensure they all get enough to eat.

Of course, you could also host your party at a restaurant and that would deal with any allergies or special dietary habits of your players, and would also ensure enough room for all of them. If this is the route you plan on going, I recommend calling in advance and getting a special room, if available.

When deciding on drinks, I always like to push for water and other healthy-ish options such as lemonade or other juices. The girls would probably appreciate a soda or two, so if you want to do that, I suggest getting a dark cola and a clear drink. That should make everyone happy.

If you are having the party at your home, I suggest getting disposable plates, napkins, and utensils. If you are cooking for them, you'll already have enough dishes to do, and there's no need to add more to the pile. If you have enough dishes and aren't worried about a glass or two getting broken, this step is optional.

Disposable plates and utensils are not optional, however, if you are catering an event. It doesn't matter how much lemonade you have, if there are no cups to put it in, you'll end up dumping it out. Also consider other items such as tables, serving plates, tongs, beverage holders or ice-filled coolers, and garbage cans and recycling bins. Walk through the food line in your mind and make sure to have everything you might need.

If the event is held at a school or restaurant, parking should not be an issue, unless you are in a big city and it costs to park (in which case, you already know to alert the families). If the party is at your home, be sure to communicate where families can park, and consider alerting your neighbors if that is common practice where you live. Having balloons or a sign in front of your house might also help parents find your home easier, and make parking less stressful.

One of the hardest challenges an awards banquet poses in my mind is entertainment. You could put together a slideshow, play videos from their matches or tournaments if you have any, or lay out newspaper clippings covering matches over the season.

Also, if you have a large yard and the weather is nice, it might be fun to put up a volleyball net for some casual volleyball. Parents and siblings might enjoy this as well.

At the very least, whether the event is held at your home, in a restaurant, at a school, or any other venue, you should include clean music while everyone is waiting for the awards to begin, a chance to eat, and a few decorations. Even if you just blow up some balloons and have them in your home, this should add to the celebratory vibe.

Finally, determine ahead of time how many guests you can expect. This will make prepping for the event ten times easier, but it is something fairly simple to overlook. After you get that number, anticipate 10-20% more may show up. It is better to be over-prepared than shorthanded.

DETERMINING AWARDS (HINT: YOUR STATS HELP!)

When deciding awards to give out, there are a few approaches you can take. One extreme is to choose all of the awards yourself, either based on judgment or by using your stats to help you out. On the other end of the spectrum is letting your players vote for winners of different awards.

I have found that assigning awards based on my own perception has led to the least amount of controversy since there is always the concern that it was "just a popularity contest" if you allow the girls to vote.

Have the girls vote on a "Team Player" award if you want to still include their opinions, and then even if it does boil down to a popularity contest, that's essentially what the award represents anyway and there should be minimal controversy.

You also need to consider what awards you actually want to give out. A few classics are "Most Valuable Player," "Coaches Award," and "Most Improved." You might also give out awards to your team captains if they were the same people for the entire season.

This format is well received and highlights accomplishments throughout the year for a variety of players. Whether you are coaching middle school, high school, club or an after-school program, giving out these awards would make for an acceptable awards banquet or celebration.

If you want to get a little more personal, you could also create more customized awards for your players. By this point you should know that I'm a big statistics fan, so I of course implement these numbers into awards at the end of the year.

For example, you could give an award for "Best Offensive Player," "Best Defensive Player," "Best Blocker," "Most Assists," "Most Digs," etc. I hear often in the media complaints that "everyone gets an award," and that it "isn't right." I don't follow this train of thought to a

CHAPTER 9: CELEBRATIONS AND AWARDS

tee, though I do agree to a certain degree.

Should a player who was a sub for the entire year get the same award as the MVP? No. Should they be recognized for their contribution to the team? Definitely. So if you have someone who you find got the most aces on your team, yet they weren't the MVP, why not still share their accomplishment with the team?

Awards and other forms of recognition can vary in their formality. Maybe you decide ahead of time that you will order trophies and get them engraved with the player's names and award titles on them. Or perhaps a certificate would better fit your team's needs.

You could mix it up a little and give trophies or certificates to the classic awards, and then give certificates or verbal acknowledgments respectively for the more specific awards.

If you are presenting your awards in front of a group which is more than just your team, remember to keep it short and sweet. Give out a few of the classic awards during this presentation, and save the personalized ones for a meeting with just your team.

We all love to talk about ourselves, yet can get bored listening to others do the same. This is especially true during awards for an entire school or club program. Give out the personalized awards either before or after the big presentation, and save the MVP, Coaches Award and Most Improved to be presented in front of everyone.

POSITIVITY ONLY

Coaches love to hear themselves talk. It's just a fact. We can talk for hours about our team, often finding we've gone down some strange tangent about our philosophy on playing time despite originally discussing our favorite plays to run or even just responding to a simple, "How's the team doing this year?"

This can get us in trouble sometimes since we just follow and share our train of thought instead of first monitoring what is about to come out of our mouths. This can be especially true during award banquets following a not-so-stellar season or a poor performance at a final match or tournament.

To avoid this black hole of self-pity and

negativity, plan out any speeches you will give ahead of time, and make sure to monitor yourself at the actual event during small talk. Do not give out awards based on negative inside jokes, no matter how funny you think they are. Your girls are attending to receive praise and celebrate the season, not to be made fun of.

Ending on a high note will leave a good last impression on your players and parents, and carry you into your next season with a positive outlook.

CHAPTER 10: FINAL THOUGHTS

A lot goes into coaching. For the first-time coach, especially if you are taking on the role of head coach, the first season can be overwhelming even for former players. There are many more administrative tasks than you might expect, but they should not intimidate you. Especially now that you've read through this guide!

The joy of coaching is so much greater than the headaches you'll face managing contact information cards, creating ref schedules, and calculating stats after every game. Although this book was based primarily on sharing the administrative tasks of coaching with you, I hope you could read through the lines and see the fun and excitement that will fill the majority of your season.

I could hardly wait to start coaching, but had a hard time finding a place to coach. Once I finally caught a break, I thought knowing how to play volleyball was enough. I had an idea of how to run practice and a clue as to how to communicate with parents, but there was so much I didn't know and had to learn the hard way.

I searched for books from the very beginning to give me an idea of what to do and expect in my first year of coaching. While there were books upon books upon books about different drills to run and the best workouts to do, I found nothing with the information I was looking for.

So, this book really is for all of the new coaches out there, no matter how much volleyball you've played. If you've never coached volleyball before, or maybe have only helped as an assistant, this will help you out tremendously. So while I've mostly avoided talking about the highs and lows of coaching, I do think they're important to address.

UPS AND DOWNS

Over the course of the season, you will

CHAPTER 10: FINAL THOUGHTS

experience ups and downs. And not just nice rolling hills ups and downs. I'm talking serious roller coaster, slow climb up to the top and then fast drop to the bottom, with a twist or two in the middle for good measure.

The downs are the scariest, so let's just get those out of the way first. You are going to be coaching anywhere from 8-12 girls for three to five months. You will see them at least once a week, probably more, and will spend full days with them at tournaments or on game days.

You're going to go into difficult competitions, and you may not always come out victorious. In fact, you might lose more than you win. This takes a toll on psyches and can impact even the most optimistic coaches, players, and parents.

But even more serious than losing here and there is the fact that life happens, and your players may go through tough personal times while they're on your team. You might find out midway through the season that one of your players has been bullied at school by some of your other players, someone has an eating disorder, or a parent is dealing with alcoholism.

A player could have a serious injury at school or

may experience a death in the family. Practice might be their escape from a less than supportive home life.

My intention here is not to bring you down. It's exactly the opposite. How great is it that you get to be someone who is there for your girls when they are going through such a hard time? You could very well be the only one who asks someone how their Spanish class is going or be the only adult they get to share a funny story with about school.

Any one of these "downs" can be turned into a positive experience where you help your players manage and move forward.

Now, we're not psychologists (well, maybe you are, but I'm not). We also need to understand boundaries based on our role in a player's life, and should make referrals or suggestions to players or parents if the situation should warrant one. But simply by building a trustworthy environment you are making yourself a safe resource for your players.

So the downs are out of the way! Let's pick it up a little.

CHAPTER 10: FINAL THOUGHTS

You are going to see tremendous growth out of your players. This is the aspect of coaching which I find most rewarding, and can actually be demonstrated by one of my favorite coaching memories.

One year of coaching, I had a 14-year-old setter who had never been challenged in her position on past teams, and after a tournament or two, I had the feeling that she just expected to have that position. She was not really pushed to grow.

My starting middle, who was just as tall, if not taller than me (I'm 5'8"), had beautiful hands. She was a natural setter, but because of her height had always played middle. Not to mention, she was also very good at that position too.

After a few tournaments with low attacking percentages, I attributed this to the fact that, as much as I hate to say it, my setter just wasn't trying very hard. I wanted to try something new, so I announced at one of our early practices that our stud middle would start practicing at setter.

Although it was not my intention, this really got

my regular setter down. Her position was threatened and it visibly upset her. I let it go and did not address it with her. The middle-turned-setter was phenomenal. I could already see our hits improving with her setting, though her understanding of the position was still a little shaky.

This change meant my previous backup setter was no longer needed, and I was now short a middle. Well… I moved my backup setter, a shy 7th grader, to middle. She was honestly the one I was most worried about in this mini-experiment of mine because her confidence had the most potential for being rattled if things didn't work out.

Our first tournament using these new positions was interesting, to say the least. There was a lot of bumping into each other, confusion over who was leading the team on the court, and maybe even some skepticism from the parents. We got through it, but it wasn't pretty.

My original setter, after moping around for a week or two about the lineup change, kicked it into high gear. She took the obstacle which was in front of her, and although it shook her at

CHAPTER 10: FINAL THOUGHTS

first, she didn't let it get the best of her. She eventually earned back her spot as the starting setter and was so much more valuable to our team with her new attitude.

My new middle, the 7th grader, actually started to excel at middle as well. This pushed someone else to outside, and she began subbing in to play middle on a regular basis, always growing in skill and confidence.

Fast forward to our regional tournament. Due to circumstances too wordy for this story, we had not been originally invited to play in the regional tournament because of our ranking. However, two teams dropped out, and we entered regionals as the #64 team, the lowest ranked team at the tournament.

We were actually a great team this year, winning practically every tournament we attended, but due to association rules hadn't been allowed to advance. What an exciting time to show off our skills and prove the association wrong!

After some serious scrambling and a lot of phone calls, we confirmed our attendance and made the long drive down to regionals, not knowing what to expect.

Picture this:

The tournament begins, and we win our first game. And our second game. And we just keep winning! We go from starting at the bottom to playing for the division championship in one day. We are playing with the possibility to end the season ranked at #33, a huge jump by any measure (literally the biggest jump possible).

So we are playing in the championship game. We came to the tournament to make a statement, and we are making it. We win the first game, and our players can feel the championship within their grasp.

But then we lose the second game. It is a stressful feeling, knowing that a win is so close, yet you must prove that you want it and deserve it more than the other team. As a coach, you have to consider at this point who is going to deal with the pressure best. Whose stats show the most consistency throughout the day? Who isn't afraid to lose. Who wants the ball? The win?

This is why I prefer making lineups as the day

CHAPTER 10: FINAL THOUGHTS

goes. Coaching is one big game of strategic moves, and sometimes you just have to go with your gut.

I decide to put in my now stud setter, who had earned her starting position in this match since her attitude change back in the beginning of the year. I also have my 7th-grade middle in. Despite her shyness in the beginning of the year, she has really grown into a confident player.

The third game is close the entire time, battling back and forth, winning a point and then giving one up. We are fast approaching 15, the score being 12-13, but we are behind. My heart still begins to pound with anxiety to this day thinking back to this exact moment.

So we are behind 12-13, a sideout and two points away from the greatest comeback that tournament has probably ever seen. The serve comes over, and we volley back and forth a few times, each team trying not to make a mistake. I vividly remember seeing a perfect pass go low and straight into my setter's hands, while my 7th-grade middle is simultaneously going in for a quick set.

My team, up until this point, had never ran a

play without me first suggesting it to them. And what a time to start! I had a mini panic attack.

The set is perfect and my middle takes a great swing, hitting it to the right back on the opposing team. They manage to pass it straight up, but eventually shank the ball and we get the point, the sideout, and the momentum which carries us to the greatest championship I've experienced.

The fact that these two players, a setter who was originally not internally motivated enough to push her limits, and a middle who was almost too timid to even be in the lineup in the beginning of the year, decided on their own to run a play in a close division championship match **WHEN WE WERE BEHIND** and believed in themselves and each other enough to actually pull it off! If that's not an "up" then I don't know what is.

There have been a number of proud coaching moments for me, but that one takes the cake. You will have moments like this too. And they will make everything worth it.

CHAPTER 10: FINAL THOUGHTS

GETTING TO YEAR TWO

Not all seasons will end on such a phenomenal note and have you ready to jump right back into coaching. That is what made that season so special for me.

Something that I think is important to discuss, is that there is a lot of turnover, especially at the younger and lower levels of coaching. If you intend to stick around with your current club, you should let your administrator or head coach know your intention to stay right away. Finding coaches can be hard at times, so let them know you are interested in returning as soon as possible.

You may also realize you were not as good of a fit as you had hoped for with your club or school team. Maybe once you started coaching 7th-graders, you realized you'd probably work better with 10th-graders or vice versa. This is totally fine and part of the process. We all have to start somewhere, and knowing where you would be a better fit will only help your next coaching experience.

If you would like to switch age levels or even

schools, reach out to a few places before completely walking away from your current assignment. While you may feel that you couldn't spend another year teaching 8th-graders how to run plays, by the time the next season rolls around you may very well be anxious to get back out there with them.

It can be tempting to wrap up your season and take a nice long mental vacation from volleyball. Pump the brakes! You have one more task before you get into that mindset. An important practice to get into at the very end of your season is to do a quick reflection of the three to five months you spent coaching.

Did you reach your goals? Or your definition of success? Were your players receptive to your instruction or do you need to make adjustments moving forward? What drills worked best and which ones would you rather never attempt to run again?

Write down a summary of your season month by month or however you see fit. This will help you prepare for your next year coaching, as you'll be able to project what issues or events may come up.

CHAPTER 10: FINAL THOUGHTS

So are you ready? Ready to dive into the world of coaching? Ready to share your love of volleyball with developing players? Ready to contribute to your community? To be a role model for your girls? Their siblings?

By stepping into the coaching role, you are going to give a lot of yourself for the betterment of your community. Expect to be exhausted, both mentally and physically. Expect to be challenged in multiple ways. Expect to devote yourself to a group of girls for a few months, and then watch them grow into independent individuals who you had an impact on.

Having reached the end of this book, you should be prepared for the majority of administrative work you will need to deal with throughout the season. I hope you continue to search out additional resources which will help you become a better coach and fully invest in yourself so that you can be better for your team.

Thank you for seeking out and reading this book, and I wish you good luck in your first season, and the many more which are sure to follow.

ABOUT THE AUTHOR

Whitney Bartiuk began coaching volleyball in the fall of 2008 for a local club team in St. Helens, Oregon as an assistant at the 14 and under level. This morphed into a pseudo-head coaching position due to scheduling issues for the head coach, and led to a string of coaching opportunities in subsequent seasons. After coaching five different teams and seeing greater success with each season, she sought to impact even more athletes at a higher level.

This mission resulted in moving across the country to Bowling Green, Ohio to attend Bowling Green State University (BGSU) where she earned her Bachelor of Science in Education degree in the Sport Management program, with a minor in Entrepreneurship. While in Bowling Green, Whitney worked for the city running an after-school volleyball program and officiated adult volleyball leagues. She also interned for a semester with a large volleyball academy in Maumee, Ohio, where she learned many administrative tasks associated with running an elite club and managing major tournaments.

Seeking the opportunity to work her way into an athletic director position for a university, Whitney completed her final internship required for graduation from BGSU with the Huskie Athletic Compliance Office at Northern Illinois University (NIU) in DeKalb, Illinois. Enjoying the analytical and fast-paced nature of athletic compliance, she decided to pursue a graduate degree to improve career prospects later on. In August of 2016, Whitney earned her Master of Public Administration degree from NIU, specializing in Strategic Public Management and Leadership.

Despite her enthusiasm for her work in athletic compliance, Whitney felt a disconnect from the student-athletes she was working so hard for.

ABOUT THE AUTHOR

Taking a leap of faith, she left intercollegiate athletics to focus on maintaining her website for new volleyball coaches, Get The Pancake, at www.getthepancake.com.

She returned to coaching, and directed her energy to creating resources for coaches to improve the sport for as many players as possible. Whitney can be reached through her website.

Made in the USA
San Bernardino, CA
02 July 2019